OUR SAVIOR
WHO PRAYS

John MacArthur
PUBLISHING GROUP
ESTBLD MMXXIII
Los Angeles
CALIFORNIA

DESIGNED BY WEKREATIVE CO.
ISBN: 978-1-883973-09-4
PRINTED IN CHINA

OUR SAVIOR WHO PRAYS

THE PRAYER THAT SECURES THE SAINTS' ETERNAL GLORY

JOHN MACARTHUR

CONTENTS

INTRODUCTION

All Scripture is God-breathed and spiritually profitable for the salvation and sanctification of every believer. Every word of God is pure truth, living and life-giving, powerful and empowering.

For over half a century, I have lived daily with the Scripture in my hands and on my mind—and preached it from the pulpit of the church—and written a series of expository commentaries on each New Testament book, totaling thirty-four volumes.

I am grateful for everyone who is willing to settle in and dig deep in reading a commentary. But only a few take on such an extensive journey, even though every aspect of the Scripture is life transforming. My desire, however, is for many to engage in such a pursuit because they will then experience the benefit and blessing of the deep dive into a biblical book.

I am certain when people have a taste of the riches of Bible exposition, they will want more. So I thought we should give them less to develop the hunger for more.

What do I mean by less?

ONE CHAPTER. ONE MONUMENTAL CHAPTER.

So, that led to the development of this series, *The Great Chapters of the Bible.* This series focuses on key portions of Scripture that establish the foundational truths of the Christian faith. The current volume, adapted from *John 12–21,* The MacArthur New Testament Commentary, considers John 17 and examines the supreme example of prayer in the life of our Lord Jesus.

I believe that exposition of the great chapters of the Bible will lead many to desire to know the rest of each book and to experience the blessing of knowing the Scripture in its fullness.

01

THE REAL LORD'S PRAYER

JOHN 17:1

Jesus spoke these things; and lifting up His eyes to heaven, He said, "Father, the hour has come; glorify Your Son, that the Son may glorify You ..." (17:1)

"A godly man cannot live without prayer," wrote the seventeenth-century English Puritan Thomas Watson. "A man cannot live unless he takes his breath, nor can the soul, unless it breathes forth its desires to God" (*The Godly Man's Picture* [repr.; Edinburgh: Banner of Truth, 1992], 88). Prayer expresses the soul's longing for God (Pss 42:1–2; 63:1; 143:6); it is the cry (Pss 34:15, 17; 86:3) of God's people to their gracious, compassionate (Ex 34:6; 2 Chr 30:9; Neh 9:17; Ps 103:8) heavenly Father (Matt 6:6, 9; 7:11).

The Bible both commands prayer (e.g., Jer 33:3; Matt 6:5–13; Luke 6:28; 18:1; Rom 12:12; Eph 6:18; Phil 4:6; Col 4:2; 1 Thess 5:17; 1 Tim 2:1, 8; 1 Pet 4:7; Jude 20) and records examples of the prayers of godly people.

In the Old Testament, Abraham prayed for his son Ishmael (Gen 17:18), for Abimelech (Gen 20:17), and for God to spare Sodom (Gen 18:23–32). Abraham's servant prayed for guidance in finding a wife for Isaac (Gen 24:12–14). When Rebekah was barren, Isaac prayed that the Lord would open her womb (Gen 25:21). Jacob prayed that God would protect him from Esau (Gen 32:9–12). Moses prayed that God would spare rebellious Israel (Ex 32:11–14, 31–32; Num 14:13–19; Deut 9:26–29), and show mercy to Miriam (Num 12:13) and Aaron (Deut 9:20). Moses' successor, Joshua, prayed after Israel's defeat at Ai (Josh 7:7–9) and asked for the sun to stand still so Israel could inflict further punishment on her enemies (Josh 10:12–14). Gideon prayed for a sign that would reveal God's will (Judg 6:36–40). Both Naomi (Ruth 1:8) and Boaz (Ruth 2:12) prayed for Ruth. Hannah prayed for a son (1 Sam 1:9–11), and Eli prayed for Hannah (1 Sam 1:17). Hannah's son, Samuel, prayed that God would forgive the people of Israel and deliver them from their enemies (1 Sam 7:5, 8), and promised to intercede for them after they foolishly demanded a king (1 Sam 12:19–23). Job prayed in humble contrition (Job 42:1–6) and asked that God would forgive his friends for their foolish counsel (vv. 8–10). David offered a prayer of thanksgiving for God's promised blessings to him and his house (2 Sam 7:18 29), pleaded with God to spare the son Bathsheba gave birth to after their adulterous affair (2 Sam 12:16), begged God to spare Israel from judgment (2 Sam 24:17), praised God for His blessings on the nation (1 Chr 29:10–18), and prayed for his son and successor, Solomon (1 Chr 29:19). Solomon prayed for God's blessing on Israel (1 Kgs 8:22–53), and for wisdom for himself (1 Kgs 3:5–9). Confronting the false prophets on Mt. Carmel, Elijah prayed that God would reveal

Himself as the only true God (1 Kgs 18:36–37), and that it would rain after a three-and-one-half year drought (vv. 41–45; cf. Luke 4:25; Jas 5:17–18). Elisha prayed, and a dead child was restored to life (2 Kgs 4:33–35). Hezekiah prayed, and God delivered His people from the invading Assyrians (2 Kgs 19:1–36). God also spared the king's life in response to his prayer for mercy (2 Kgs 20:1–6).

In perhaps the most unusual circumstances in which anyone ever prayed, Jonah cried out to God from the stomach of a large fish (Jonah 2:1–10). In the waning days of the southern kingdom (Judah), Jeremiah's prayer resulted in the comforting promise that God would one day restore the nation from captivity (Jer 32:17–25). During the exile, Ezekiel cried out to God to have mercy on His people (Ezek 9:8; 11:13), as did Daniel in his magnificent prayer recorded in Daniel 9:3–19. After the exile, Ezra (Ezra 8:21; 9:5–15) and Nehemiah (Neh 1:4–11) prayed for the remnant who returned to their homeland. In addition to those specific prayers, virtually the entire book of Psalms consists of prayers of various types (e.g., praise, worship, confession, petition, and thanksgiving).

The New Testament also records the prayers of God's people. After His ascension, Jesus' followers returned to Jerusalem, where they "were continually devoting themselves to prayer" (Acts 1:14; cf. 2:42). When faced with persecution by the Jewish leaders, the early church's response was to pray (4:24–31). The apostles defined their ministry when they told the congregation, "But we will devote ourselves to prayer and to the ministry of the word" (6:4). While "Peter was kept in the prison ... prayer for him was being made fervently by the church to God" (12:5, 12). Peter and John prayed for the believers in Samaria (8:14–15); Peter prayed before raising Tabitha from the dead (9:40) and before his vision and the coming of the messengers from Cornelius (10:9); the church at Antioch prayed before sending Paul and Barnabas on their missionary journey (13:1–3); and Epaphras labored in prayer for the Colossians (Col 4:12).

From his conversion (Acts 9:11) to the end of his life, Paul's ministry was marked by continual prayer (e.g., Acts 14:23; 16:25; 20:36; 21:5; 22:17; 27:35; 28:8, 15; Rom 1:8–10; 10:1; 1 Cor 1:4–8; 2 Cor 13:7, 9; Eph 1:16–23; 3:14–19; Phil 1:3–4, 9–11; Col 1:3, 9–14; 1 Thess 1:2; 3:10; 2 Thess 1:11–12; 2 Tim 1:3; Phlm 4–6). The apostle also frequently asked others to pray for him and his ministry (e.g., Rom 15:30; 2 Cor 1:11; Eph 6:18–19; Phil 1:19; Col 4:2–3; 1 Thess 5:25; 2 Thess 3:1; Phlm 22), as did the writer of Hebrews (Heb 13:18).

But the supreme example of prayer in Scripture comes from the life of the Lord Jesus Christ. Curtis C. Mitchell writes, "Beyond doubt the greatest examples of correct prayer practice ever displayed were those demonstrated by Jesus Christ. So distinct was His prayer life that by simply observing it our Lord's disciples were motivated to request instruction on the subject (see Luke 11:1)" (*Praying Jesus' Way* [Old Tappan, NJ: Revell, 1977], 15).

From beginning to end, Jesus' earthly ministry was marked by frequent times of prayer. He prayed at His baptism (Luke 3:21), during His first preaching tour (Mark 1:35; Luke 5:16), before choosing the twelve apostles (Luke 6:12–13), before feeding the 5,000 (Matt 14:19), after feeding the 5,000 (Matt 14:23), before feeding the 4,000 (Matt 15:36), before Peter's confession of Him as the Christ (Luke 9:18), at the transfiguration (Luke 9:28–29), for some children brought to Him (Matt 19:13), after the return of the seventy (Luke 10:21), before giving the Lord's Prayer (Luke 11:1), before raising Lazarus from the dead (John 11:41–42), as He faced the reality of the cross (John 12:28), at the Last Supper (Matt 26:26–27), for Peter (Luke 22:31–32), in Gethsemane (Matt 26:36–42), from the cross (Matt 27:46; Luke 23:34, 46), with the disciples He encountered on the road to Emmaus (Luke 24:30), and at the ascension (Luke 24:50–51).

But of all the prayers of Jesus, the one recorded here in the seventeenth chapter of John's Gospel is the most profound and magnificent. Its words are plain, yet majestic; simple, yet mysterious. They plunge the reader into the unfathomable depths of the inter-

Trinitarian communication between the Father and the Son, and their scope encompasses the entire sweep of redemptive history from election to glorification, including the themes of regeneration, revelation, illumination, sanctification, and preservation. The veil is drawn back, and the reader is escorted by Jesus Christ into the Holy of Holies, to the very throne of God.

The value of its infinite richness is heightened by its uniqueness. There is no other chapter in the Bible like it. As one commentator explains:

> This chapter embraces the longest recorded prayer of our Lord while He was on earth. No doubt He prayed other prayers as lengthy as this, for we know He spent much time in prayer and in communion with His heavenly Father; but God did not see fit to give these other prayers to us as the Holy Ghost spoke to holy men. We have many of the sermons of Jesus, many of His parables; but only this one lengthy prayer. (Oliver Greene, *The Gospel According to John* [Greenville, SC: The Gospel Hour, 1966], 3:132)

The setting of this prayer (as Jesus comforted His disciples immediately before the cross), the substance of it (as a heartfelt petition from the Son to the Father), and the length and detail of it, as well as its theological richness, contribute to its unique and unsurpassed significance.

THE SETTING OF THIS PRAYER

Jesus spoke these things; and lifting up His eyes to heaven, He said, "Father, the hour has come ..." (17:1*a*)

Jesus' prayer marks the end of the disciples' time with Jesus in the upper room. During the previous few hours, Jesus had served, comforted, and instructed His anxious followers. They had experienced John's fitting description of Jesus firsthand, that He "loved His own who were in the world, He loved them to the end" (13:1). The evening began with a footwashing, in which Jesus Himself "poured water into the basin, and began to wash the disciples' feet and to wipe them with the towel with which He was girded" (13:5). Remarkably, He even knowingly washed the feet of the one who would betray Him, Judas Iscariot.

Next there was the final meal, the Last Supper (cf. Matt 26:26–29; Mark 14:22–25; Luke 22:19–20; 1 Cor 11:23–26), during which Jesus revealed that Judas would betray Him (John 13:26–27; cf. Matt 26:20–25), that He was about to die (John 13:31–35), and that Peter would deny Him (John 13:36–38; cf. Matt 26:30–35). The disciples were understandably shocked and dismayed by what Jesus told them. Yet, the Lord was quick to console them, comforting them with the promise of future glory. "Do not let your heart be troubled," He said to them. "Believe in God, believe also in Me. In My Father's house are many dwelling places; if it were not so I would have told you; for I go to prepare a place for you" (14:1–2). The Lord further encouraged His followers with the promise of the Holy Spirit, the Helper who would come to them after He left. "The Helper, the Holy Spirit, whom the Father will send in My name," declared Jesus, "He will teach you all things, and bring to your remembrance all that I said to you" (14:26). Though the world would hate them, just as it hated Christ (15:18–16:4), the Spirit would strengthen and guide them in the truth (15:26–27; 16:5–15).

The words of Christ in the upper room also emphasized the vital, saving relationship that His disciples (and by extension, all believers) enjoyed with Him. Using the imagery of a vine and its branches, Jesus emphasized the abiding and life-giving nature of His love (15:1). Those who truly believe in Him share in that love, resulting in spiritual fruit (15:5), powerful prayer (15:7), a God-exalting life (15:8), heartfelt obedience (15:10; cf. 14:15), supernatural joy (15:11), and a sincere love for others (15:12). Jesus' remarkable words, "You did not choose Me but I chose you, and appointed you that you would go and bear fruit, and that your fruit would remain, so that whatever you ask of the Father in My name He may give to you" (15:16), comforted the disciples by confirming their genuine, saving relationship to Him.

Though they would grieve for a short time, Jesus assured them that their sadness was only temporary. With solemn certainty, He told them, "Truly, truly, I say to you, that you will weep and lament, but the world will rejoice; you will grieve, but your grief will be turned into joy" (16:20). The disciples, of course, did not understand that Jesus would rise from the dead only three days after the horrifying events that were about to take place (16:18; cf. John 2:22). They did not realize that His death was a necessary part of God's plan, and had been for the Messiah all along (cf. Isa 53:1–12; Dan 9:26). Their thinking, in keeping with the mainstream Jewish understanding of their day, had no place for a crucified Christ (cf. 1 Cor 1:23). The Messiah, they thought, would come, overthrow Rome, and establish His earthly kingdom. When Jesus triumphantly entered Jerusalem just a few days before, the disciples must have been overwhelmed and overjoyed (12:12–19). Though their Master was still disliked by the religious leaders (11:16, 47–53), His popularity with the people seemed to be growing (cf. 12:9–11). The crowds had jubilantly hailed Him as their king, even laying down palm branches before Him, and greeting Him with shouts of "Hosanna!" as He entered the city (12:12–18). Surely, the disciples must have reasoned, the kingdom was finally at hand.

Now, just a few days later, they were shocked to hear Jesus tell them the unthinkable—He was leaving them (13:33; 14:18; 16:16). Rather than conquering Rome, He was going away. Rather than building up a kingdom, He was laying down His life (15:14). In the upcoming hours, He would be betrayed (18:2), arrested (18:12), put on trial (18:19), abandoned (18:25–27; cf. 16:32), falsely accused (18:38; 19:4), beaten (19:1), mocked (19:5), and crucified (19:16). The disciples' great expectations quickly turned to shock, heartbreak, and despair.

It is in this context, after **Jesus spoke** the **things** recorded in the previous three chapters, that He graciously and fervently prayed for His disciples. As they left the upper room and started their journey through the city and across the Kidron Valley to Gethsemane, the disciples would have been unable to separate this prayer from the solemn instruction they had just received in the upper room. In fact, much of what Jesus had just told them is repeated in His prayer to the Father:

> This prayer clearly belongs with the farewell discourses because it reiterates and sums up various of the themes found in these discourses: (1) the departure of Jesus (vv. 11,13); (2) the joy of the disciples (v. 13); (3) the hatred of the world (v. 14); (4) the division of the world and the disciples (v. 16); (5) the truth (v. 17); and (6) the indwelling of Christ in the believers (v. 23). (Ben Witherington III, *John's Wisdom* [Louisville: Westminster John Knox, 1995], 268)

The Lord had told His disciples what to expect (14:29), and warned them of the persecution they too would face on His behalf (15:18). He had comforted them with the promise of heaven (14:2) and of the Holy Spirit's coming (14:16–17). He had assured them of His love for them, and of their saving relationship with Him (15:1–11). He had instructed them with regard to their love for one another (15:12, 17), and even modeled that love in washing their feet (13:1–20). Now He would model that sacrificial love once again—this time by publicly praying for them, entrusting their safekeeping to His Father.

The Lord had promised them peace, joy, strength, provision, answered prayer, spiritual power through the Holy Spirit, and intimate fellowship both with Himself and the Father. All of those promises culminated in Christ's concluding promise that the disciples would triumph over the world: "These things I have spoken to you, so that in Me you may have peace. In the world you have tribulation, but take courage; I have overcome the world" (16:33). It is no coincidence that this prayer immediately follows that exultant declaration. Having stated His victory over the world, Jesus immediately turned in submissive dependence to the One who would ensure His triumph. "To transform the victory which was announced into a present reality, nothing less was needed than the action of the omnipotence of God. It is to Him that Jesus turns" (Frederic Godet,

Commentary on John's Gospel [repr.; Grand Rapids: Kregel, 1978], 883).

The circumstances were certainly dismal from a human perspective, just hours before the cross. Yet Jesus' prayer was anything but pessimistic. Instead, it was a confident declaration of undying faith and certain glory. In the words of Leon Morris,

> We so often understand this prayer as though it were rather gloomy. It is not. It is uttered by One who has just affirmed that he has overcome the world (16:33), and it starts from this conviction. Jesus is looking forward to the cross, but in a mood of hope and joy, not one of despondency. (Leon Morris, *The Gospel According to John*, The New International Commentary on the New Testament [Grand Rapids: Eerdmans, 1995], 634)

Jesus began His prayer by **lifting up His eyes to heaven,** a familiar posture (cf. 11:41; Ps 123:1; Mark 6:41; 7:34) acknowledging God's throne in heaven. It also reflected the confidence of His pure heart (Matt 5:8; Eph 3:12; cf. the guilt-stricken tax collector's unwillingness to lift up his eyes to heaven [Luke 18:13]). By addressing God as **Father** (cf. vv. 5, 11, 21, 24, 25; Matt 11:25–26; 26:39, 42; Luke 10:21; 23:34, 46; John 11:41; 12:28), Jesus acknowledged His submission to and dependence on Him, while simultaneously underscoring His equality with God as His Son (cf. John 5:18). In contrast to the common Jewish practice of referring to God with a plural pronoun, "our Father," Jesus addressed Him as "My Father" (e.g., Matt 7:21; 10:32–33; 11:27; 12:50; 16:17; 18:10, 19; 20:23; 26:39, 42; Luke 22:29; John 5:17; 6:32, 40; 8:19, 38, 49, 54; 10:18, 29, 37; 14:7, 20, 21, 23; 15:1, 8, 15, 23, 24; 20:17). Gerald Borchert explains the cultural significance of that personal title:

> Jesus came into a Jewish world that had developed a remote view of God, one that needed angels to carry messages. The people had ceased to use the name of God for fear of taking his name in vain, just like the Prodigal Son, who could speak of "heaven" but not use the name of God (cf. Luke 15:18, 21). Into this context of speaking of God by means of surrogate titles Jesus came and called God his Father. (Gerald L. Borchert, *John 12–21*, The New American Commentary [Nashville: Broadman & Holman, 2002], 187)

In addressing this prayer to His Father, Jesus emphasized the intimate fellowship He shared with God. That kind of a personal, familial relationship with God was completely foreign to the Jews of Jesus' day. Yet through Christ, anyone who believes in Him is granted that same spiritual intimacy with God (17:20, 26).

That Jesus referred to God as His Father is significant for another reason. On the one hand, He was "making Himself equal with God" (John 5:18) by claiming to be the Son of God. But on the other hand, He was demonstrating His distinctness from the Father, since He was clearly not praying to Himself. That twofold reality underscores an important theological truth—that the Son is equal to the Father yet distinct from Him. Thus, while He is equal to the Father in essence, even sharing in His eternal glory (17:5), He is not a mere mode or manifestation of the Father. Rather, the Son is a distinct person within the Godhead. By calling God His Father, Jesus was underscoring the fundamental reality of the Trinity.

Earlier in John's gospel the point had been emphasized that Christ's hour had not yet come (2:4; 7:6, 30; 8:20). But now He opened His prayer with the dramatic declaration that **the hour has come.** The phrase refers to the consummation of His earthly ministry, encompassing His death, resurrection, and ascension.

The unfolding drama of redemptive history had reached its apex. Plans made in eternity past were finding their culmination in time. The hour had come in which the Son of Man would offer Himself as the perfect and only atoning sacrifice for sin. The hour had come when the sinless One would be made sin for believers that they "might become the righteousness of God in Him" (2 Cor 5:21). The hour had come when Christ would cancel "the certificate of debt consisting of decrees against us, which was hostile to us" taking "it out of the way, having nailed it to the cross"

(Col 2:14). This was the hour when the Old Testament prophecies of Messiah's death would be fulfilled; when the serpent's head would be bruised (Gen 3:15); when the suffering Servant, "a man of sorrows and acquainted with grief" (Isa 53:3), would be "pierced through for our transgressions ... crushed for our iniquities" and have "the chastening for our well-being [fall] upon Him [so that] by His scourging we are healed" (v. 5). It was the hour when the shadows of the Old Testament sacrifices (cf. Heb 10:1) would give way to the glorious reality of the final sacrifice—the Lamb of God (John 1:29; Heb 10:14). It was the hour of Christ's triumph over the prince of this world and the kingdom of darkness (John 12:31; 16:11; Col 2:14; Heb 2:14). It was the climactic hour when God, through Christ's sacrifice, would defeat sin, death, and Satan, and redeem a people for Himself.

With the hour of supreme suffering and even greater victory at hand, and with His terrified and heartbroken disciples still surrounding Him (cf. 18:1), the Lord lifted His eyes to heaven and prayed. Though the words of this prayer would be magnificent in any context, the palpable imminence of the cross makes Christ's plea as poignant as it is profound.

THE SUBSTANCE OF THIS PRAYER

"glorify Your Son, that the Son may glorify You." (17:1*b*)

Having acknowledged that the time of His death was near, Jesus immediately requested that the Father would **glorify** the **Son,** so **that the Son may glorify** the Father. This short phrase (which will be discussed in more detail in the following chapter of this commentary) provides a fitting summary to all that had taken place in Jesus' life and ministry, and to all that was to follow both in this prayer and in the events of His passion. His prevailing focus had always been on glorifying His Father, perfectly submitting to the Father's will in everything, even to the end.

Throughout His ministry, Jesus was continually "seeking the glory of the One who sent Him" (John 7:18; cf. 13:31–32). The events of His birth brought glory to God (Luke 2:14, 20); as did His teaching (Matt 5:16; John 15:8); His miracles (Matt 9:8; 15:31; Mark 2:12; Luke 5:25–26; 7:16; 13:13; 17:15; 18:43); and His death and resurrection (John 12:23–28). In absolutely everything, the Son had submitted to the Father's will. "For I have come down from heaven," He explained to the crowds, "not to do My own will but the will of Him who sent Me" (John 6:38; cf. Matt 12:50; John 4:34; 5:30). Even during His passionate prayers in

Gethsemane, when the temptation to abandon the cross was at its peak, Jesus submitted to the plan of God. "My Father, if it is possible, let this cup pass from Me," He prayed, "yet not as I will, but as You will" (Matt 26:39; cf. v. 42). Just as the Son had glorified the Father, so the Father had glorified the Son. Thus, Jesus could say to His opponents, "The Father who sent Me, He has testified of Me" (John 5:37), and later, "It is My Father who glorifies Me, of whom you say, 'He is our God'" (John 8:54). At His baptism, the Father audibly affirmed His approval of the Son (cf. Matt 3:13–17). This occurred a second time at His transfiguration (cf. Luke 9:35; 2 Pet 1:17–18), and a third time shortly before His passion (John 12:28). The Father further demonstrated that Jesus was truly His Son through His miracles (John 2:11; 9:3; 10:38; 11:40); as Jesus said regarding Lazarus's death, "This sickness is not to end in death, but for the glory of God, so that the Son of God may be glorified by it" (John 11:4). Even the events of Jesus' death and resurrection would result in the glory of the Son (Luke 24:46; John 12:23; 13:32)—glory that He has shared with the Father since eternity past (John 1:1, 14) and that will be visibly displayed to the world at His future return (Matt 16:27; Mark 8:38; Luke 21:27).

It is fitting that His ministry would climax in a majestic prayer that emphasized the very thing that characterized His entire life. The theme of God's glory, stated in verse 1, is echoed throughout this passage. Just as the Son glorified the Father through His faithfulness on earth (17:4), so the Father would glorify the Son together with Himself, with the very glory that the Son shared with Him since before time began (17:5). The disciples too would be those who glorified the Father by bringing glory to the Son (17:10); they, along with all who would believe in the Son, would share in His glory (17:22), eternally praising Him for the glory that He received from the Father (17:24). Furthermore, the plan of salvation would certainly be fulfilled in the cross since God's glorious reputation, His name, was at stake (cf. 17:6, 11, 12, 26).

The prayer itself falls readily into three sections, as Jesus prays for Himself (vv. 1–5), His disciples (vv. 6–19), and His church (vv. 20–26). But throughout all three sections, the focal point is the glory of God, being manifested through the cross. As Frederic Godet explains,

> When Jesus prays for Himself [in vv. 1–5], it is not His own person that He has in view, it is *the work of God* ... ; when He prays for His apostles [in vv. 6–19], He commends them to God as agents and continuers of this work; and when He extends His regard to all believers present or future [in vv. 20–26], it is as if to the *object* of this work, in other terms because these souls are the theatre where the glory of His Father is to shine forth; for His work and the glory of the Father are for Him one and the same thing. (*Commentary on John's Gospel*, 883)

Ironically, it was through the cross, the most shameful of deaths, that the Son of God displayed infinite glory. What seemed to be the worst possible outcome for Jesus, at least in the minds of His disciples, was in reality His ultimate victory. By looking at the cross from the standpoint of God's glory, the Lord saw triumph where His followers saw nothing but tragedy.

Jesus' prayer highlights His absolute confidence in and submission to the perfect will of God, even though He knew perfectly what it would cost Him. Therefore, He prayed that the Father's will would be done, that the master plan of redemption would be accomplished, and that the Father would bring to reality all the promises He had made to His disciples. Knowing the will of God did not cause Jesus to fatalistically forego praying. On the contrary, it prompted Him to ask the Father to do what He had said He would do (cf. Daniel's prayer in Dan 9:4–19, which was prompted by his understanding from Jeremiah's prophecy that Israel's captivity would last for seventy years [Dan 9:2–3]). Not only did Jesus impart the truth to His disciples, but He also prayed that God would energize it in their lives. Teaching the truth must always be coupled with prayer; a lesson that the disciples themselves would later put into practice (Acts 6:4).

The prayer recorded in this chapter also forms a transition between Jesus' earthly ministry and His heavenly ministry of intercession (Heb 7:25). The book of Hebrews reveals the rich theological truths regarding the Lord's intercessory work as the mediator of the new covenant (cf. Heb 4:14–10:25); here we have a personal glimpse of Him in His role as the Great High Priest interceding for His people. (This prayer is, in fact, often referred to as the High Priestly Prayer of Christ.) Significantly, as was noted earlier, this is the only place in Scripture where the words of a lengthy prayer of Christ have been recorded. Though shorter prayers can be found (cf. Matt 11:25–27), there is no parallel in Scripture to the prayer recorded here.

Yet, in spite of its unique character and profundity, Jesus' words are simple and straightforward. No amount of study could ever exhaust the truths revealed in this prayer; and yet a basic understanding and appreciation of the text comes just from reading and meditating on it. One might expect the words of an inter-Trinitarian prayer to be utterly incomprehensible. But that is not the case. As James Montgomery Boice rightly observes:

> This prayer contains the simplest of sentences, though the ideas are profound. It is proof that the difficulty we have in understanding God's truth is not in the complexity of the truth itself or in the language with which it is conveyed (as if it were logarithms or German philosophy) but in our own ignorance, sin, and spiritual lethargy. (James Montgomery Boice, *The Gospel of John* [Grand Rapids: Zondervan, 1985], 1103)

Because He was consumed with the glory of God, as the substance of His prayer makes clear, Jesus viewed the cross from an eternal perspective. He was not dispassionate or stoic (cf. Luke 22:42), but fully dependent on His Father's care and wholly submissive to His will. Perfectly aware of the pain and suffering that awaited Him, He also knew of the triumphant glory that would result. Thus, "for the joy set before Him [He] endured the cross, despising the shame," knowing that He would soon victoriously sit "down at the right hand of the throne of God" (Heb 12:2).

THE SIGNIFICANCE OF THIS PRAYER

Spoken by Jesus just hours before the cross, the significance of this passage is difficult to overstate. Here the words of the second member of the Trinity are recorded, as He speaks to His Father about the nature of their communion, about the outworking of their eternal plan of salvation, and about the way in which the disciples and all believers fit into that plan. In hearing this prayer, the disciples were allowed to listen in on the most holy and profound of conversations. In reading this prayer, believers today are similarly ushered into the Holy of Holies, where they find their Great High Priest—even in the moments before His death—interceding on their behalf. Some refer to it as the "Holy of Holies of sacred Scripture."

Though the church has always cherished and meditated on this prayer, and though individual Christians have studied it in great detail, its rich truths have never been exhausted. Hundreds of sermons have been preached on it, thousands of pages written about it, and millions of lives changed by it. And the words of the Lord remain as relevant and meaningful today as they were when He first uttered them.

> Its primary characteristic is *timelessness*. Though uttered within a few hours of Calvary, it contains thoughts and expressions which must have been familiar to our Lord at any moment during the centuries which have followed. As we study it, therefore, we are listening to words which have been uttered many times on our behalf, and will be uttered until we are with Him, where He is, beholding the glory of the divine Son, superadded to that of the Perfect Servant. (F. B. Meyer, *Gospel of John* [Grand Rapids: Zondervan, 1952], 296. Emphasis in original.)

In light of the fact that this prayer is the longest and, arguably, most significant of Jesus' recorded prayers, it is ironic that the title, "The Lord's Prayer" has traditionally been used elsewhere, in reference to the instruction on prayer in Matthew 6:9–13 (cf. Luke 11:2–4). Yet Matthew 6:9–13 does not actually record a prayer of Jesus, but rather is a model given by Jesus to His disciples for how they should pray—a disciple's prayer would be a better title. (Jesus, after all, could never have asked God for forgiveness—cf. Matt 6:12.) If one wishes to read an actual prayer of the Lord, at least a prayer of any length, this passage is the only place to turn. From that perspective, the prayer recorded in John 17 is the true Lord's Prayer.

As Jesus prayed this prayer shortly before the cross, He rejoiced, knowing that the redemption that had been predetermined in eternity past was about to find its terminus in time and space. Jesus understood that the hour had finally come for the fulfillment of that which God had promised from before time began. He was ready to face the cross—with triumph and resolve. The cost would be immense, but the glorious result would be eternal.

02

JESUS' PRAYER AND THE ETERNAL PLAN OF GOD

JOHN 17:1b–5

"Father, the hour has come; glorify Your Son, that the Son may glorify You, even as You gave Him authority over all flesh, that to all whom You have given Him, He may give eternal life. This is eternal life, that they may know You, the only true God, and Jesus Christ whom You have sent. I glorified You on the earth, having accomplished the work which You have given Me to do. Now, Father, glorify Me together with Yourself, with the glory which I had with You before the world was." (17:1*b*–5)

Though unthinkable to the disciples, the death of the Messiah was an essential and deliberate part of God's eternal plan. Even though Jesus had told them clearly that "the Son of Man is going [up to Jerusalem to be killed] as it has been determined" (Luke 22:22), they did not fully understand what He meant (Mark 9:32; Luke 9:45). Moreover, they objected to what little they did understand—as this startling scene from Matthew's gospel demonstrates:

> From that time Jesus began to show His disciples that He must go to Jerusalem, and suffer many things from the elders and chief priests and scribes, and be killed, and be raised up on the third day. Peter took Him aside and began to rebuke Him, saying, "God forbid it, Lord! This shall never happen to You." But He turned and said to Peter, "Get behind Me, Satan! You are a stumbling block to Me;

> for you are not setting your mind on God's interests, but man's." (Matt 16:21–23)

It was not until after the resurrection that the disciples finally understood why Christ's death was necessary—in order that He might be the perfect substitute for sin, reconciling sinners to God through the cross (2 Cor 5:18–21). Only then did the disciples come to realize that His death had been central to the divine plan all along. On the day of Pentecost, none other than Peter announced that Jesus Christ was "delivered over by the predetermined plan and foreknowledge of God [being] nailed to a cross by the hands of godless men" (Acts 2:23). His sentiments were echoed in the apostolic prayer of Acts 4:27–28: "For truly in this city [Jerusalem] there were gathered against Your holy servant Jesus, whom You anointed, both Herod and Pontius Pilate, along with the Gentiles and the peoples of Israel, to do whatever Your hand and Your purpose predestined to occur" (Acts 4:27–28). In fact, the reason the Old Testament prophets had been able to predict the Messiah's death with such vivid accuracy was because it had been part of the divine plan from the beginning (Acts 3:18; cf. Gen 3:15; Isa 53:1–12; Dan 9:26; 1 Pet 1:20–21).

The salvation plan of God was formed in eternity past, before the beginning of time, when He purposed to save a remnant of the human race He would yet create and whom He knew would rebel against Him (Eph 1:4–5; cf. Matt 25:34). The plan itself was guaranteed by the promise of God. As Paul explains in Titus 1:2, salvation is "the hope of eternal life, which God, who cannot lie, promised long ages ago." The phrase "long ages ago" literally means, "before time began," indicating that redemption has always been part of God's sovereign plan (cf. Heb 13:20). In eternity past, He made a promise to save those whom He had chosen; the fulfillment of which is absolutely certain since "it is impossible for God to lie" (Heb 6:18; cf. Num 23:19; 1 Sam 15:29; John 14:6, 17; 15:26). But to whom was that promise made, since there was no one but God before time began?

The answer to that question is introduced in 2 Timothy 1:9, which states that God "has saved us and called us with a holy calling, not according to our works, but according to His own purpose and grace which was granted to us in Christ Jesus from all eternity." (The phrase "from all eternity" is identical in Greek to the phrase translated "long ages ago" in Titus 1:2. In both cases, the literal rendering is "from before time began.") God's promise to save His own was made in eternity past "according to His own purpose and grace," independent of any outside influence. Because there was no one beside the triune God, it was a promise He necessarily made to Himself.

More specifically, as Jesus' beautiful prayer in this chapter indicates, this divine promise was made from one member of the Trinity to another—from the Father to the Son. As a tangible expression of His infinite love for the Son, the Father promised Him a bride (cf. Rev 19:7–8), a company of redeemed sinners who would honor and glorify the Son forever. In eternity past, the Father recorded their names in the book of life (Rev 13:8; 17:8), and pledged them to His Son as a gift of His love. Thus, Jesus could pray, "Father, glorify Me together with Yourself, with the glory which I had with You before the world was. I have manifested Your name to the men whom You gave Me out of the world; they were Yours and You gave them to Me" (17:5–6). A few verses later, Jesus again underscored that believers are a gift from the Father, given out of His love and for the purpose of His Son's glory: "Father, I desire that they also, whom You have given Me, be with Me where I am, so that they may see My glory which You have given Me, for You loved Me before the foundation of the world" (v. 24).

Earlier in the gospel of John, Jesus had already made reference to the fact that believers are given to Him by His Father. After He fed the five thousand, He told the crowds, "All that the Father gives Me will come to Me, and the one who comes to Me I will certainly not cast out.... This is the will of Him who sent Me, that of all that He has given Me I lose nothing, but raise it up on the last day" (John 6:37, 39). He further taught that "No one can come to Me unless the Father who sent Me draws him" (v. 44). According to God's sovereign design, the Father draws to the Son those whom He has chosen to redeem, in keeping with His eternal promise. The Son, in return, receives and protects all those whom the Father draws. Because they are a gift to Him from the Father, He would never refuse them or allow them to be lost. He will raise them all to eternal glory.

Sinners, then, are saved not because they are inherently worthy of salvation, or wise enough on their own to choose it (cf. Eph 2:1–10), but because the Father lovingly draws them for the purpose of giving them as a gift to the Son. In response to the Father's love, the Son eagerly receives all those who are drawn because they are a gift from His beloved Father. The Son opens His arms to sinners, not because they either deserve to be embraced or seek such, but because He is exceedingly glad to receive the gift His Father prepared for Him from before time began, and then sought and saved.

Romans 8:29–30 provides additional insight into the glorious salvation purposes of God: "For those whom He foreknew, He also predestined to become conformed to the image of His Son, so that He would be the firstborn among many brethren; and these whom He predestined, He also called; and these whom He called, He also justified; and these whom He justified, He also glorified." When the Father, in eternity past, decided to redeem sinners, He did so with the ultimate intent of conforming them into the image of His Son (cf. Phil 3:20–21; 1 John 3:2). Because they will be like Christ in their glorified state, the redeemed will forever be a supreme tribute to the Son—reflecting His perfect goodness and proclaiming His eternal greatness.

First Corinthians 15:24–28 foretells the remarkable conclusion to God's sovereign plans. There Paul writes,

> Then comes the end, when He [Christ] hands over the kingdom to the God and Father, when He has abolished all rule and all authority and power. For He must reign until He has put all His enemies under His feet. The last enemy that will be abolished is death. For He has put all things in subjection under His feet. But when He says, "All things are put in subjection," it is evident that He is excepted who put all things in subjection to Him. When all things are subjected to Him, then the Son Himself also will be subjected to the One who subjected all things to Him, so that God may be all in all.

The day is coming when Jesus Christ, the true Lord of Lords, will reclaim the universe that rightfully belongs to Him. He will reign by His Father's authority until He subjects every enemy to Himself, including death (vv. 25–26). When that takes place, at the end of time, the Son will hand His kingdom back over to His Father (v. 24), and will Himself "be subjected to the One [the

Father] who subjected all things to Him, so that God may be all in all" (v. 28). The Son will give everything, including Himself and those who are in Him, back to His Father. Thus, the Father's love gift to the Son will be reciprocated by the Son, and the redemptive purposes of God, which were formed in eternity past, will be fully and finally realized. God will be "all in all" (v. 28) and salvation history will be complete.

The humbling but marvelous reality is that believers are secondary within the scope of God's eternal plan. The Father's primary concern is the honor of the Son whom He loves and desires to see glorified. That is why, in eternity past, He promised to redeem a segment of sinful humanity whom He would give to the Son to worship and exalt Him forever.

The Son's primary concern, likewise, is the honor and glory of the Father. Because of His perfect love for the Father, He receives the Father's gift with infinite joy—gladly embracing every sinner whom the Father draws. Moreover, He considered the Father's gift so precious that He "emptied Himself, taking the form of a bond-servant, and being made in the likeness of men. Being found in appearance as a man, He humbled Himself by becoming obedient to the point of death, even death on a cross" (Phil 2:7–8). He did this that the eternal purposes of God might be fulfilled in Him (cf. Eph 3:11)—purposes that will finally culminate when He gives all things back to His

Father at the end of the age (1 Cor 15:25–28). (For a further discussion of this subject, see my foreword, "Divine Immutability and the Doctrines of Grace," in Steven J. Lawson, *Foundations of Grace* [Orlando, FL: Reformation Trust, 2006], 7–20.)

It is with these eternal purposes in mind that Jesus came to His Father in prayer on the night before His death. He knew that the Father had predetermined to redeem a people whom He would give to the Son as His bride. He also knew that the redeemed would reflect His glory (John 17:22; Phil 3:20–21; 1 John 3:2), bear His image (Rom 8:29), and praise, glorify, and serve Him through all eternity. Likewise, He knew that their names were written in the Book of Life (Phil 4:3; Rev 3:5; 13:8; 17:8; 20:15; 21:27), and that He had come into the world to pay the redemptive price to purchase them from the slave market of sin (1 Cor 6:20; 7:23; Titus 2:14; 1 Pet 1:18; Rev 5:9). He was fully aware that **the hour** had **come** for Him to do all that had been planned from before the foundation of the world.

Thus when Jesus asked the Father, **glorify Your Son,** He was asking that the eternal plan of redemption be consummated exactly as it had been sovereignly ordained. Significantly, this was Jesus' only request for Himself in His entire prayer (cf. v. 5)—that the Father would grant Him the glory that would be His through His death, resurrection, ascension, and coronation, just as it had been planned in eternity past. The fact that the Son shares the Father's glory affirms His deity, since God will not give His glory to another (Isa 42:8; 48:11).

The Lord's request was a sincere affirmation of the promise His Father had made to Him in eternity past. The plan had always been that the Son would be glorified through the redemption of sinners. Thus Jesus' request for glorification was a prayer that God's eternal purposes would be fulfilled in the cross exactly as God had decreed. Ironically, what would appear to men to be a moment of supreme shame would in actuality be the moment of Christ's highest honor—as God's marvelous plan of redemption was perfectly realized. In fact, it is through the cross that all of God's saving purposes are made possible. Jesus will forever bear the scars of the cross (John 20:27), thus being forever marked with the honor of His accomplishment there.

But Jesus was not merely seeking His own glory; His perfectly righteous request was that by His sacrifice **the Son** might **glorify** the Father (cf. Rom 6:4). As Leon Morris explains,

> This part of the prayer is often said to be Jesus' prayer for himself. As he prays that he may be glorified (vv. 1, 5) there is perhaps something in this. But this is not prayer "for" himself in the way we usually understand this. Since his glorification is to be seen in the cross it is a prayer rather that the Father's will may be done in him. If we do talk about this as Jesus' prayer for himself we should at least be clear that there is no self-seeking in it. (Leon Morris, *The Gospel According to John,*

The New International Commentary on the New Testament [Grand Rapids: Eerdmans, 1995], 635)

The cross displayed God's glory like no other event in history, revealing His righteousness, justice, and holiness in requiring the "precious blood" of His Son, "a lamb unblemished and spotless" (1 Pet 1:19) as a propitiation for His holy wrath against sin (Rom 3:25). At the same time, it dramatically demonstrated His grace, mercy, and love in the sending of His only Son to die for the sins of the utterly undeserving (Eph 2:1–10; cf. 1 John 4:9–10). "What God has accomplished in Jesus Christ," notes Thomas Schreiner, "displays both the justice and love of God because God's holiness is vindicated in the cross, while at the same time his love is displayed in the willing and glad sacrifice of his Son" (Thomas R. Schreiner, "Penal Substitution View," in *The Nature of the Atonement: Four Views*, ed. James Beilby and Paul R. Eddy [Downers Grove, IL: InterVarsity, 2006], 92). The cross further displayed God's power as He defeated sin, death, and Satan (Heb 2:14; cf. 1 Cor 15:54–58). Finally, the cross made clear the wisdom of God's eternal plan of redemption—"the wisdom which none of the rulers of this age has understood; for if they had understood it they would not have crucified the Lord of glory" (1 Cor 2:8).

In these opening expressions, Jesus referenced four facets of the saving purposes of God, each of which centered on His glory-producing work of redemption at the cross—the right He possesses (to offer eternal life); the relationship He offers (which is eternal life); the requirement He meets (to pay for eternal life); and the reverence He deserves (having made eternal life available). As His prayer indicates, Jesus was fully aware that, like everything else, the next few hours of time had been sovereignly determined since eternity past and would have infinite ramifications into eternity future.

THE RIGHT HE POSSESSES

"even as You gave Him authority over all flesh, that to all whom You have given Him, He may give eternal life." (17:2)

In keeping with God's eternal plan of salvation, the Son was given **authority over all flesh** (mankind) to grant eternal life **to all** those **whom** the Father had **given Him.** That authority, being granted to Him by His Father, was made possible through the cross. Though He submitted to His captors and allowed Himself to be nailed to a cross by wicked men, in reality it was He who had the authority. In dying for the sins of those who would believe in Him, He was given the right to grant eternal life to them.

> Jesus, the Son of Man who is about to be glorified and thus will fulfill his earthly mission, here anticipates his exalted, authoritative position subsequent to his crucifixion and resurrection. This authority enables him to bestow eternal life on all those whom God has given to him (cf. 6:39–40). God's granting of authority to Jesus (cf. 1:12; 5:27) marks the inbreaking of a new era (cf. Isa 9:6–7; Dan 7:13–14). All authority in heaven and on earth has been given to Jesus (Matt 28:18), including the authority to judge (John 5:27). (Andreas Köstenberger, *John*, Baker Exegetical Commentary on the New Testament [Grand Rapids: Baker, 2004], 486)

Though His authority extends over all creation (cf. Matt 28:18), it is clear that redemption applies only to those who have been chosen for Him by the Father. Only those whom the Father has given Him (vv. 6, 9, 24; 6:37, 39; cf. Acts 13:48; Rom 8:29–30; Eph 1:4–5; 2 Thess 2:13; Titus 1:1; 1 Pet 1:1–2) will receive eternal life. Christ's authority to grant them that life is another aspect of His victory over the world through His death (cf. 16:33). That Jesus Christ is the source of eternal life is a central theme of John's Gospel (cf. 3:15–16, 36; 4:14; 5:21, 24, 40; 6:27, 33, 35, 40, 47, 48, 51, 54, 68; 10:10, 28; 11:25; 14:6 and the apostle's purpose statement for writing his Gospel in 20:31), and one he reiterates in his first epistle (1 John 5:20).

Throughout His ministry, Christ manifested the divine authority His Father had given Him in a multitude of ways (cf. Matt 11:27; 28:18). His teaching was characterized by divine authority (Matt 7:29; Mark 1:22; Luke 4:32); as were His healings (Mark 5:38–43; Luke 4:39; 9:1; John 11:43), exorcisms (Matt 10:1; Mark 3:15; Luke 4:36), and other miracles (cf. Mark 8:26–27; Matt 21:19; John 21:3–11). He claimed the right to violate traditional Jewish customs (cf. Matt 5:21–22, 27–28; 15:1–9; Luke 6:1–11; John 5:9–17), to cleanse the temple (cf. Matt 21:12–13; Mark 11:15–17; John 2:14–16), to forgive sins and offer salvation in His own name (Matt 9:6, 8; Mark 2:10; Luke 5:24), to receive worship from others (Matt 14:33; 15:25; 28:9), and even to judge the world (Mark 13:26–27; John 5:22–23). It was because His authority clashed with that of the Jewish religious leaders that they were so often angered by Him, and ultimately plotted His death.

His death, too, was under His own authority. As He declared in John 10:17–18, "For this reason the Father loves Me, because I lay down My life so that I may take it again. No one has taken it away from Me, but I lay it down on My own initiative. I have authority to lay it down, and I have authority to take it up again. This commandment I received from My Father." As the time of His crucifixion approached, Jesus did not relinquish the authority that His Father had given to Him. Rather, He anticipated the full authority He would have as a result of the cross. Following His resurrection, He knew that He would ascend to heaven where His Father would seat "Him at His right hand in the heavenly places, far above all rule and authority and power and dominion, and every name that is named, not only in this age but also in the one to come. And He [would] put all things in subjection under His feet, and [would give] Him as head over all things to the church" (Eph 1:20–22).

The fact that Jesus Christ alone was given the authority to grant eternal life, through His death on the cross, also underscores the exclusivity of the gospel message. It is only through Him that eternal life can be received. As Jesus had said earlier that evening, "I am the way, and the truth, and the life; no one comes to the Father but through Me" (John 14:6). Though many may claim to offer eternal life (Matt 7:13–14; 24:5), only the Son has actually been given the authority to grant it. As John the Baptist explained, "The Father loves the Son and has given all things into His hand. He who believes in the Son has eternal life; but he who does not obey the Son will not see life, but the wrath of God abides on him" (John 3:35–36).

THE RELATIONSHIP HE OFFERS

"This is eternal life, that they may know You, the only true God, and Jesus Christ whom You have sent." (17:3)

In contrast to the pluralistic claims of contemporary religious culture, eternal life comes only to those who **know** (the Greek word implies not mere intellectual knowledge, but a deep, intimate love relationship; cf. v. 25; 10:14–15, 27) **... the only true God** (Jer 10:10; 1 Thess 1:9; 1 John 5:20; cf. 1 Cor 8:6) and that is possible only through **Jesus Christ whom** He has **sent** (cf. 5:23, 36, 37; 10:36; 1 John 4:10, 14). As Peter boldly declared to the Jewish leaders, "There is salvation in no one else, for there is no other name under heaven that has been given among men by which we must be saved" (Acts 4:12; cf. 1 Tim 2:5).

The essence of **eternal life** is participation in the blessed, everlasting life of Christ (cf. 1:4) through union with Him (Rom 5:21; 6:4, 11, 23; 1 Cor 15:22; 2 Cor 5:17; Gal 2:20; Col 3:3–4; 2 Tim 1:1, 10; Jude 21). It is the life of God in the soul of man (Gal 2:20). Because believers have Christ's life in them, they also possess His peace (John 14:27; 16:33; cf. Phil 4:7), love (John 15:10; cf. Rom 5:5), and joy (John 15:11). The life that God predetermined to give the redeemed is a life of shared communion with Him.

Eternal life refers to a quality of life, and not just a quantity of life. It is much more than living forever; it is enjoying intimate fellowship with God both now and forever. It cannot be reduced merely to endless existence, since the unredeemed in hell will also live forever (cf. Matt 25:46 where the same word, *aiōnios*, describes both the eternal life of the righteous and the eternal punishment of the wicked).

Because eternal life is a quality of life, it is not only a future possession, but also a present reality. In John 5:24 Jesus said, "Truly, truly, I say to you, he who hears My word, and believes Him who sent Me, has eternal life, and does not come into judgment, but has passed out of death into life." "These things I have written to you who believe in the name of the Son of God," John wrote, "so that you may know that you have eternal life" (1 John 5:13). Thus, believers enjoy eternal life even now as they experience the rich blessings that come through their personal and intimate fellowship with Christ (John 15:1–11; 1 Cor 1:9; Eph 1:3; Phil 3:8–11; 1 John 1:3; 5:20). Of course, they will most fully experience that life in the age to come (Eph 2:6–7), when they see Christ face-to-face (1 Cor 13:12) and worship Him in the perfect, unending glory and joy of heaven (Rom 8:19–23, 29; 1 Cor 15:49; Phil 3:20–21; 1 John 3:2; Rev 22:3–4).

THE REQUIREMENT HE MEETS

"I glorified You on the earth, having accomplished the work which You have given Me to do." (17:4)

In God's perfect plan, and in keeping with His perfect justice, the Son had to come to earth in order to save those whom the Father had given Him (Luke 19:10). As was noted earlier, the Father's gift was so precious to the Son that He was willing to do whatever was necessary to receive it (cf. Phil 2:1–11).

The Lord Jesus Christ **glorified** the Father during His time **on the earth** by **having** perfectly **accomplished the work which** the Father gave Him to do (cf. 4:34; 5:30; 6:38; 15:10). That work culminated in the cross, which He viewed here in an anticipatory way. Jesus was certain that the eternal promise of God would be perfectly accomplished, and that nothing could prevent the Father's purposes from being realized. But His statement did more than merely reveal His own confidence in the plans of the Father. It also served as an example to the disciples—reminding them to trust in God's sovereign working and take comfort in knowing that He was in control.

Additionally, this verse implies the truth of Christ's impeccability (sinlessness). "Which one of you convicts Me of sin?" Jesus boldly challenged His adversaries (John 8:46). Paul described Him in

2 Corinthians 5:21 as "Him who knew no sin." The writer of Hebrews declared that though He was "tempted in all things as we are," Jesus was "yet without sin" (Heb 4:15), and went on to characterize Him as "holy, innocent, undefiled, separated from sinners" (Heb 7:26). Peter referred to Him as "a lamb unblemished and spotless" (1 Pet 1:19) and declared that He "committed no sin" (1 Pet 2:22). John said simply, "In Him [Christ] there is no sin" (1 John 3:5). Most significant of all was the Father's affirmation, "This is My beloved Son, in whom I am well-pleased" (Matt 3:17; 17:5). Only by living a sinless life could Jesus be an acceptable sacrifice for sin.

When John the Baptist hesitated to baptize Him, Jesus told him, "Permit it at this time; for in this way it is fitting for us to fulfill all righteousness" (Matt 3:15). It was imperative for Him to live a life of perfect obedience, fulfilling all of God's righteous requirements. Only One who was perfectly holy, just as God is holy (Lev 19:2), could be the final sacrifice for sin (cf. Heb 10:1–18). Through His death and resurrection, Jesus conquered death and provided eternal life to all who believe in Him. But in addition, His perfect life of obedience, the fullest expression of which was His willingness to die on the cross (Luke 22:42), is imputed to believers at justification (cf. Rom 5:18–21). Though Jesus was sinless, God treated Him as if He had committed the sins of everyone who would believe in Him, so that believers, though unrighteous, could be treated as if they had lived Christ's perfect life. Again, 2 Corinthians 5:21 succinctly summarizes that glorious truth: "He [the Father] made Him [Christ] who knew no sin to be sin on our behalf, so that we might become the righteousness of God in Him." Christ's willingness to be a sin-bearing sacrifice on the cross was the ultimate demonstration of His complete commitment to obey the Father, as well as the ultimate expression of His love for sinners (cf. John 15:13).

THE REVERENCE HE DESERVES

"Now, Father, glorify Me together with Yourself, with the glory which I had with You before the world was." (17:5)

Having accomplished everything according to the predetermined plan of God, Jesus knew that He would be exalted to the place where He had been before His incarnation—at the glorious right hand of His Father (cf. Mark 16:19; Eph 1:20). With that exaltation in sight, Jesus expressed His desire to return to the glory of heaven. Therefore He asked the Father to **glorify** Him, **together with** the Father, **with the glory** He had shared with the Father **before the world was.** The apostle John described the eternal fellowship Christ had enjoyed with the

Father in the prologue to his gospel: "In the beginning was the Word [the Son], and the Word was with (lit. 'face-to-face with') God, and the Word was God. He was in the beginning with God" (John 1:1–2). After an earthly life of submission and humiliation during the incarnation, Jesus was ready to return to the full glory that awaited Him at the Father's right hand. It was time for His coronation, which Paul described in Philippians 2:9–11:

> For this reason also, God highly exalted Him, and bestowed on Him the name which is above every name, so that at the name of Jesus every knee will bow, of those who are in heaven and on earth and under the earth, and that every tongue will confess that Jesus Christ is Lord, to the glory of God the Father.

Jesus looked beyond the humiliation and suffering in obedience, His death on the cross (Phil 2:5–8), to the glory that awaited Him upon His return to heaven. The glory He would receive was rightfully His, both by His divine title (as the second member of the Trinity) and by His perfect submission (since He had submitted to His Father perfectly). He also knew that His death would bring eternal life to all who would believe in Him, thus causing joy in heaven (Luke 15:7, 10) and adding voices to the eternal choir of those who will praise and worship Him forever. The contemplation of those marvelous realities enabled Him to rejoice in the cross, even though He despised the shame of bearing sin (Heb 12:2) and the horror of being forsaken by the Father (Matt 27:46).

As those on the other side of the cross, removed from it by nearly two thousand years, believers must never lose sight of the glory and honor Christ deserves because of His redemptive work. What He endured on the cross is now the anthem of Christian praise and worship. And it will be for all of eternity, as believers forever praise the Lamb who was slain (Rev 5:9). Though the Gospels record His earthly life and ministry—including the agony and suffering of His passion—it must always be remembered that He is no longer on the cross or in the tomb. He is even now the glorified Son of God, seated at His Father's right hand in power and glory (Rev 1:13–20; cf. Dan 7:13–14). The joy of seeing and praising Him in triumph awaits all those who love Him, while all who reject Him will be rejected by Him (Matt 7:23; 25:41).

The glorious truth is that the cross made eternal life possible for all who sincerely believe in Jesus Christ (Rom 10:9–10), and even before the cross all who genuinely repented of sin and trusted the forgiveness and mercy of God as their only hope (cf. Isa 55:6–7). Were it not for the cross, there would be no salvation from sin for anyone in any age, no gospel of grace, no hope for this life, and no eternal destiny but hell. Without the cross, the eternal plan of salvation that God promised from before the beginning of time would never have come to fruition. The contemplation of those truths should cause everyone who knows and loves the Lord Jesus Christ to say with the apostle Paul, "But may it never be that I would boast, except in the cross of our Lord Jesus Christ, through which the world has been crucified to me, and I to the world" (Gal 6:14).

03

JESUS PRAYS FOR HIS DISCIPLES—PART 1: AS THOSE WHOM THE FATHER HAD GIVEN HIM

JOHN 17:6–10

"I have manifested Your name to the men whom You gave Me out of the world; they were Yours and You gave them to Me, and they have kept Your word. Now they have come to know that everything You have given Me is from You; for the words which You gave Me I have given to them; and they received them and truly understood that I came forth from You, and they believed that You sent Me. I ask on their behalf; I do not ask on behalf of the world, but of those whom You have given Me; for they are Yours; and all things that are Mine are Yours, and Yours are Mine; and I have been glorified in them." (17:6–10)

The doctrines of divine sovereignty (that God elected sinners for salvation in eternity past) and human responsibility (that sinners are held accountable for how they respond to the gospel) are both clearly taught in Scripture, and play an important role in this passage.

Without apology or excuse, the Bible teaches that the Father "chose [believers] in Him [Jesus Christ] before the foundation of the world" (Eph 1:4; cf. Col 3:12; Titus 1:1; 2 John 1). In eternity past, they were "predestined" for justification (Rom 8:29), adoption (Eph 1:5), and a heavenly inheritance (Eph 1:11). Based on no merit or work of their own (Eph 2:8; Titus 3:5), God "saved [believers] and called [them] with a holy calling, not according to [their] works, but according to

His own purpose and grace which was granted [them] in Christ Jesus from all eternity" (2 Tim 1:9). Thus, they are "beloved by the Lord, because God has chosen [them] from the beginning for salvation" (2 Thess 2:13). Credit for their salvation is wholly based on the Father's gracious electing choice, made possible through the Son's sacrificial death. The reality is that they would have remained "dead in [their] trespasses and sins" (Eph 2:1), if God had not imparted spiritual life to them (v. 4). The Lord Himself declared that "No one can come to Me unless the Father who sent Me draws him" (John 6:44), underscoring the sinner's utter inability to come to saving faith unless God sovereignly initiates that work in his or her heart. Salvation is never the result of human morality, wisdom, or willpower, but of God's gracious purposes. As Paul told the Romans, salvation "does not depend on the man who wills or the man who runs, but on God who has mercy.... [And] He has mercy on whom He desires, and He hardens whom He desires" (Rom 9:16, 18). Though Paul preached the gospel to thousands, only "as many as had been appointed to eternal life believed" (Acts 13:48). No one outside of those whom God has preselected for salvation will ever embrace Jesus Christ as Savior (cf. Rom 3:10–12; 9:11; 1 Thess 1:3–4; 1 Pet 1:2).

At the same time, the Bible contains numerous entreaties to all unsaved people to believe in the Lord (e.g., Isa 55:1; Matt 11:28–30; John 5:40; 7:37–39; Rev

22:17). The gospel call, "Believe in the Lord Jesus, and you will be saved" (Acts 16:31), goes out as an open invitation to every sinner. The gracious offer is the same for everyone everywhere: "If you confess with your mouth Jesus as Lord, and believe in your heart that God raised Him from the dead, you will be saved" (Rom 10:9). In fact, God's expressed desire (which is different than His sovereign decree) is for "all men to be saved and to come to the knowledge of the truth" (1 Tim 2:4). That desire is made manifest in the gospel call, which extends to all people (Matt 28:19), and which reveals the grace of God by offering salvation to anyone who believes in Jesus Christ (cf. Titus 2:11). The truth is that "many are called, but few are chosen" (Matt 22:14), meaning that while the gospel is a plea to all men everywhere to repent (Acts 17:30), only the elect will embrace it in faith. Yet those who reject the gospel do so willingly and without excuse (cf. Rom 1:20), having been given ample opportunity to respond by their patient Creator and Judge (2 Pet 3:9; cf. Rev 2:21). On the basis of their own willful sins (Rev 20:12–13; cf. Matt 16:27), which evidence the fact that their names were never written in the Book of Life (Rev 20:15; cf. 13:8; 17:8), they will be justly condemned and sent to eternal destruction (cf. 20:14; Matt 25:46; 2 Thess 1:9).

In this way, Scripture presents the dual realities that God is absolutely sovereign in choosing who will be part of His redeemed people, and also that sinners who reject the gospel bear personal responsibility for refusing God's offer of salvation. To be sure, there is an element of mystery (from the human perspective) in how those two truths work together in the mind of God. But believers should not go beyond what has been revealed in Scripture in trying to reconcile what their finite minds are incapable of comprehending (cf. Deut 29:29; 1 Cor 4:6); if both truths are set forth in God's Word, then both should be embraced. Furthermore, sinful human beings dare not accuse God of unfairness in only electing some sinners to salvation—since, if God were fair, all sinners would experience His wrath (cf. Rom 3:23; 6:23). No one has the right to question the eternal saving purposes of God. Anticipating any such reactions, the apostle Paul responded firmly with these words:

> You will say to me then, "Why does He still find fault? For who resists His will?" On the contrary, who are you, O man, who answers back to God? The thing molded will not say to the molder, "Why did you make me like this," will it? Or does not the potter have a right over the clay, to make from the same lump one vessel for honorable use and another for common use? What if God, although willing to demonstrate His wrath and to make His power known, endured with much patience vessels of wrath prepared for destruction? And He did so to make known the riches of His glory upon vessels of mercy, which He prepared beforehand for glory, even us, whom He also called, not from among Jews only, but also from among Gentiles. (Rom 9:19–24)

Believers will praise God for all eternity because He graciously chose them and redeemed them through the work of the Son. They did nothing to earn their salvation, and therefore all the glory goes to God. But those who reject the gospel and are condemned to hell will have no one to blame but themselves. Having willfully suppressed the truth in unrighteousness, they will receive the penalty they rightly deserve for their rebellion. The seventeenth-century English Puritan Richard Baxter graphically illustrated this point in his classic work, *The Saints' Everlasting Rest*:

> [Salvation] was dear to Christ, but free to us.... Here is all free; if the Father freely give the Son, and the Son freely pay the debt; and if God freely accept that way of payment, when he might have required it of the principal; and if both Father and Son freely offer us the purchased life on our cordial acceptance; and if they freely send the Spirit to enable us to accept; what is here, then, that is not free? O the everlasting admiration that must surprise the saints to think of this freeness! ... What an astonishing thought it will be [in heaven] to think of the immeasurable difference between our deservings and receivings! Between the state we should have been in, and the state we are in! To look down upon hell, and see the vast difference from that to which we are adopted! What pangs of love will it cause within us to think, "Yonder was the place that sin would have brought me to; but this is it that Christ hath brought me to! Yonder death was the wages of my sin, but this eternal life is the gift of God, through Jesus Christ my Lord.... But no thanks to us, nor to any of our duties and labors, much

> less to our neglects and laziness; we know to whom the praise is due and must be given for ever.... So then let DESERVED be written on the door of hell; but on the door of heaven and life, THE FREE GIFT. (*The Practical Works of Richard Baxter* [repr.; Grand Rapids: Baker, 1981], 14–15)

The eternal saving purposes of God had always been Jesus' primary concern during His earthly ministry (Luke 5:31–32; 19:10; John 3:16–17; 4:34–38). Now, as the cross drew near, the Lord articulated those purposes in this magnificent prayer to His Father—voicing them audibly so that His disciples could hear. The Lord knew that what had been planned in eternity past would be fulfilled in the next few hours of time (cf. vv. 1–5). He also knew that His disciples would abandon Him at the critical moment (John 13:36–38; 16:32), that their faith would be shaken (cf. Luke 22:31–32), and that their hearts would be deeply grieved (John 16:22). Though His own suffering would far outweigh theirs, Jesus sacrificially served them (as He had done throughout His entire ministry [cf. Mark 10:44–45] including that evening [John 13:1, 12], and would ultimately do on the cross [15:13]) by praying for them. In fact, of the twenty-six verses that comprise Jesus' prayer in John 17, fourteen center specifically on the disciples (vv. 6–19) with an additional seven (vv. 20–26) focusing on those who would believe in Christ in the future through their extended ministries.

Having prayed that the Father would glorify the Son (in vv. 1–5), Jesus then interceded for His disciples (vv. 6–19). This section of His High Priestly Prayer may be discussed under two headings: His prayer for them as those whom the Father had given Him (vv. 6–10); and His specific requests for them in light of His imminent departure (vv. 11–19). The first of those headings will be discussed below, with the second being addressed in the following chapter.

The frightening realization that Christ was leaving them was a paralyzing thought to the disciples. They had depended on Him for everything. He had been their teacher (John 13:13), their protector (Matt 12:1–5), and the supplier of all their needs (cf. Luke 22:35). But now He was going away. They were about to be left alone and, from their viewpoint, thrown back on their own resources. Understanding their fears, Jesus spent much of His time with the disciples on the evening before His death comforting them. He reassured them that He would continue to love them and provide for their needs (see the exposition of chapters 13–16 in *John 12–21*, The MacArthur New Testament Commentary). Now, having given the disciples those marvelous promises, Jesus prayed that the Father would ensure those promises. As one commentator explains:

> By far the largest part of Jesus' prayer relates to the disciples. He was much more concerned about them than about himself. He

> was sure of the suffering that was inevitable and the victory that was certain. The disciples, however, were a variable quantity; in themselves they were likely to fail.... Nevertheless, he prayed for them with confidence that they would be kept by the Father's power and presented for a future ministry. (Merrill C. Tenney, "The Gospel of John," in *The Expositor's Bible Commentary*, ed. Frank E. Gaebelein [Grand Rapids: Zondervan, 1981], 9:163)

Jesus' confidence was founded, not in the resolve of the eleven, but in the will and power of the Father. But before launching into His specific requests for the disciples (in vv. 11–19), the Lord explained why He knew the Father would honor His requests (in vv. 6–10).

Verse 6 serves as an important transition statement from Christ's prayer for His own glory (in vv. 1–5) to His prayer for the disciples (in vv. 6–19). Of note in this verse is the interplay between the human side and the divine side of salvation. Christ subsequently expanded on each of those topics, as He established the disciples' believing response on the one hand (in vv. 7–8), and God's sovereign election on the other (in vv. 9–10). The verse itself provides a thesis statement of sorts for the verses that follow, introducing the reasons why Jesus knew the Father would ensure His previous promises to the disciples (in chapters 13–16) and answer His subsequent requests for them (in vv. 11–19).

The Lord defined those for whom He was praying first of all as those to whom He had **manifested** the Father's **name.** The phrase connects back to verse 4, indicating that part of Christ's earthly mission was to make known the Father's name to the disciples. **Manifested** translates a form of the verb *phaneroō*, which means "to reveal," "to make known," or "to show." The aorist tense denotes that this was an accomplished fact, one that Christ had perfectly finished according to the Father's plan. The concept of God's **name** encompasses all that He is: His character, nature, and attributes. Psalm 9:10 reads, "Those who know Your name will put their trust in You, for You, O Lord, have not forsaken those who seek You." In Psalm 20:7 David exulted, "Some boast in chariots and some in horses, but we will boast in the name of the Lord, our God," while in Psalm 22:22 he declared, "I will tell of Your name to my brethren" (cf. 5:11; 8:1; 48:10; 75:1; 115:1; 119:55; 1 Kgs 8:33, 35, 43, 44, 48; 1 Chr 17:24; 2 Chr 6:20; Neh 1:11; Isa 26:8, 13; Mic 6:9).

The supreme manifestation of the name of God was the Lord Jesus Christ, God in human flesh. So perfectly and completely did Jesus reveal God's nature and character that He could make the shocking statements, "He who sees Me sees the One who sent Me" (John 12:45) and, "He who has seen Me has seen the Father" (14:9; cf. 1:18). The New Testament writers declare Him to be "the image of the invisible God, the firstborn of all creation" (Col 1:15), in whom "all the fullness of Deity dwells in bodily form" (2:9), "who ... existed in the form of God" (Phil 2:6) and "is the radiance of His glory and the exact representation of His nature" (Heb 1:3).

The name of God was so sacred to the Jews that they refused to pronounce it. Instead, they took the consonants from the tetragrammaton (YHWH; cf. Ex 3:14–15) and added the vowels from the word *adonai* ("Lord"). When they read the Hebrew text of the Old Testament, they pronounced the resulting word ("Yahweh," rendered "Jehovah" in older English translations) "Adonai," in order to avoid speaking God's name aloud. Jesus, however, not only manifested God's name, He spoke it. And even more shockingly, He took it for Himself (cf. John 8:24, 58 and the exposition of those verses in *John 1–11*, The MacArthur New Testament Commentary [Chicago: Moody, 2006]). In so doing, Jesus so outraged His Jewish opponents, who thought it blasphemy, that they sought to kill Him (John 5:18; 8:59; 10:31–33), and eventually succeeded (John 19:7).

Nonetheless through His death, Jesus Christ opened the way to personal, loving fellowship with God. As He Himself said, "I am the way, the truth, and the life; no one comes to the Father but through Me" (John 14:6). And earlier, using the metaphor of a sheepfold, He declared, "I am the door; if anyone enters through Me, he will be saved, and will go in and out and find pasture" (John 10:9). Those who have placed their faith in Him have their sins forgiven, and enjoy an intimate relationship with the Father, whom they have the privilege of calling Abba (Rom 8:15; Gal 4:6), which endearingly means, "Papa" or "Daddy."

Christ further described the disciples to the Father as **the men whom You gave Me out of the world** (cf. 15:19). The truth that believers are a gift from the Father to the Son has already been seen as an important theme in this prayer (cf. vv. 2, 9, 24). The **world** is the evil, godless, satanically ruled system composed of all the unredeemed and all that opposes God and His kingdom (cf. 7:7; 12:31; 14:17, 19, 30, 31; 16:11; 2 Cor 4:4; Eph 6:12; 1 John 5:19). Christians are no longer part of the world, having been "rescued ... from the domain of darkness, and transferred ... to the kingdom of His beloved Son" (Col 1:13). Earlier that evening, Jesus had told the disciples, "If the world hates you, you know that it has hated Me before it hated you. If you were of the world, the world would love its own; but because you are not of the world, but I chose you out of the world, because of this the world hates you" (15:18–19). Since they are no longer part of it, and indeed have been crucified to it (Gal 6:14), believers are not to be conformed to the world (Rom 12:2) or walk in it as they once did (Eph 2:2; cf. 1 John 2:15–17). Instead, they are called to overcome it (1 John 5:4–5) by keeping themselves unstained by it (Jas 1:27) and avoiding friendship with it (Jas 4:4).

Christ's statement **they were Yours and You gave them to Me** is a forceful affirmation that even before their conversion the disciples belonged to God. Earlier in John's Gospel, the Lord had declared, "All that the Father gives Me will come to Me, and the one who comes to Me I will certainly not cast out" (6:37; cf. v. 39; 17:2, 9, 24). God told the apostle Paul that He had "many people in this city [Corinth]" who belonged to Him even though they were not yet saved (Acts 18:10; cf. 13:48). As was discussed earlier, God elected believers to salvation in eternity past (Eph 1:4), and wrote their names in the Book of Life (Phil 4:3; Rev 13:8; 17:8; 20:12, 15; 21:27; 22:19; cf. Dan 12:1; Luke 10:20). Having chosen to redeem them, the Father gave them to the Son as gifts of His love (see the fuller discussion of this glorious reality in the previous chapter of this volume). Thus, as earlier demonstrated, the disciples (and by extension all believers—cf. v. 20) were infinitely precious to the Son, not because of anything intrinsically valuable in them, but because they were promised to Him by His Father before time began (cf. 2 Tim 1:9; Titus 1:1). As the next few hours would prove, Jesus considered the Father's gift so precious He was willing to die to receive it.

In addition to recognizing that they were a gift from His Father, the Lord also described the disciples as those who **have kept** the Father's **word.** That statement introduces the element of obedience essential to salvation (cf. Phil 2:12–13). That obedience, of course, is not a meritorious work that contributes something to salvation (cf. Gal 2:15–16), but is rather the inevitable result of genuine saving faith (cf. Eph 2:8–10). Thus, to say that the disciples had obeyed the Father's Word is merely another way of expressing that their faith was genuine. The New Testament inseparably joins saving faith and obedience, so much so that obedience is often used as a synonym for faith (e.g., John 3:36; Acts 6:7; Rom 1:5; 16:26; 1 Pet 1:2). It is also the sure mark of sincere love for Jesus Christ (John 14:15, 21, 24; 15:10, 14). (Interestingly, Jesus used forms of this same Greek word for "keep" (*tereō*) in vv. 11, 12, 15 when He asked the Father to keep the disciples. Thus, the Lord asked the Father to keep those who keep His Word.)

The disciples, then, were among those who kept the Word that had been revealed to them. From the heart, they had responded in genuine faith to the truth they had received. At the same time, Scripture recognizes that they had done so because they were a gift from the Father to the Son, having been among those whom He sovereignly chose in eternity past and called effectually in time for salvation. The rest of this section (vv. 7–10) builds on those inseparable twin truths. Having summarized them in verse 6, Jesus continued to explain why He knew the Father would grant His requests regarding the disciples: because they had believed in Him as the Son (vv. 7–8) and because they were a gift to Him from the Father (vv. 9–10).

BECAUSE THEY HAD BELIEVED IN HIM AS THE SON

"Now they have come to know that everything You have given Me is from You; for the words which You gave Me I have given to them; and they received them and truly understood that I came forth from You, and they believed that You sent Me." (7:17–18)

Though they had been with Jesus for several years, it was not until **now** that His disciples were beginning to truly understand the mission His Father had given Him. It would still be a few days until Christ arose, when they would begin to fully grasp the reasons Jesus had to die. Yet they clearly believed that Jesus was whom He claimed to be (Matt 16:16; Mark 8:29; Luke 9:20), that He came from the Father, and that He alone spoke the words of eternal life (cf. John 6:68–69). As Jesus had already stated in verse 6, they had kept His Word and thus had proven to be His true disciples (cf. John 8:31).

The content of the disciples' faith offers further proof of its genuineness. Though before the cross there was still much that they did not grasp, they sincerely believed the truths they did understand (in contrast to the false faith of many others—cf. John 2:23–25; 6:64, 66). The eleven had **come to know** first of all, as Jesus said to the Father, **that everything You have given Me is from You** (a statement that again highlights His intimacy with and dependence on the Father). The disciples believed that Jesus worked by the power of God and did everything according to His Father's will. This was in contrast to the Jewish religious leaders, who accused Jesus of operating through the power of Satan (Matt 12:24). Such conclusions, as Christ Himself pointed out, were not only blasphemous and unforgivable (cf. Matt 12:24–32) but foolish, since Satan would never empower someone to further the work of God (vv. 25–29). The disciples, of course, knew the truth. They had seen Jesus' miracles, which were marked by divine compassion (Matt 14:14; 15:32; 20:34; Mark 1:41; 6:34; 9:35–36; Luke 7:13–14); they had heard Jesus' sermons, which pierced the heart with divine authority (Matt 7:29; 13:54; 22:33; Mark 1:22; 6:2; 11:18; Luke 4:32; John 7:46); they had seen Jesus pray, knowing that He spent long hours in communion with His Father (Matt 14:23; Mark 1:35; Luke 5:16; 6:12; 9:18, 28; 11:1–4); they had watched Jesus' minister to sinners, and yet never sin Himself (Matt 9:11; 11:19; Luke 5:29–32; 15:2; 1 Pet 2:22; 3:18; 1 John 2:29; 3:5); they had even witnessed the Father's visible and audible approval of His Son (Matt 17:5; Mark 9:7; Luke 9:35; John 12:28; cf. Matt 3:17). They knew that He came from God, and as a result they followed Him wholeheartedly (Matt 19:27; cf. Mark 8:34; Luke 9:57–62; John 12:25–26).

The disciples likewise believed that **the words which** the Father **gave** to Jesus were true (cf. v. 14;

7:16; 8:28; 12:49; 14:10, 24). Jesus had **given** those words **to them; and they received them,** by both affirming them and subsequently acting upon them (cf. Jas 1:22). They **truly understood** Christ's divine origin, **that** He **came forth from** the Father (cf. 16:30). **They** also **believed** in His divine mission, **that** the Father had **sent** Him into the world (cf. vv. 18, 21, 23, 25; 3:34; 4:34; 5:24, 30, 36, 37; 6:38, 39, 44, 57; 7:16, 28, 29, 33; 8:16, 18, 26, 29, 42; 9:4; 11:42; 12:44, 45, 49; 13:20; 14:24; 15:21; 16:5; 20:21). They had come to realize what John's prologue articulates: that He is the Son of God (John 1:1; cf. 16:30), equal in essence and eternally coexistent with the Father (1:1–2), the Creator of all things (1:3), and the source of eternal life and spiritual light (1:4). They recognized the glory of the Word made flesh, and knew that it was "glory as of the only begotten from the Father, full of grace and truth" (1:14). Soon they would also understand the wonders of His death and resurrection (cf. 16:20). Those realizations were revolutionary for the disciples:

> The response of these men did not seem like very much. But for them to see the source of these things was a spiritual miracle more wonderful than the miracle of a man born physically blind being enabled, for the first time, to see the wonder of a tree, the glory of a sunset, the mobile mystery of a human face. (John Phillips, *Exploring the Gospel of John* [Grand Rapids: Kregel, 1989], 321–22)

After Pentecost, the proof of their faith would be demonstrated in dramatic ways, as they boldly proclaimed Jesus as Lord to all who would listen. Though they suffered severe persecution and (for nearly all of them) martyrdom, the disciples would not abandon what they knew to be true. Even the threat of death could not undermine the undying conviction that God had placed within them (cf. Acts 4:13; 5:41). The saving faith they were given was enduring by its very nature (cf. 1 Pet 1:3–9; 1 John 2:19).

Through their obedience, they demonstrated that they were among those whom the Father had elected as a love gift for His Son. Their works did not save them, but they did evidence that true saving faith was alive in their hearts. James Montgomery Boice posed the question,

> How does one tell who are the elect of God? How do we judge who are Christians and who are not? ... There is only one answer, the answer given by the Lord Jesus Christ [speaking] of those who were truly his disciples [in John 17:6–8]. According to these verses, the only way to tell whether one is a Christian or not is to see whether he or she believes and continues in the words of the Lord Jesus Christ. (*The Gospel of John* [Grand Rapids: Baker, 1999], 1276)

The Bible teaches that God will certainly bring to glorification all those whom He predestined in eternity past (cf. John 6:37, 39; 10:28; Rom 8:29–30;

Eph 1:13–14; Phil 1:6; 1 Thess 5:23, 24; 1 Pet 1:5; Jude 1, 24). It also teaches that those whom God has truly chosen will respond in faith to the gospel, and will also persevere in the truth to the end (cf. Matt 24:13; 1 Cor 15:1–2; Col 1:21–23; Heb 2:1; 3:14; 4:14; 6:11–12; 10:39; 2 Pet 1:10). On the one hand, this perseverance requires diligent effort on the part of believers (Phil 2:12; 1 Tim 4:7–8; Heb 5:9). On the other hand, it is a work that God ultimately does through believers (Phil 2:13; Heb 13:21). In fact, all of the Christian life (including the desire to pursue godliness) is a result of God's grace (cf. 1 Cor 15:10; 2 Cor 3:5). (Note the discussion in the following chapter of this commentary regarding God's power to protect the faith of those who are His.)

As those who had received, believed, and persevered in the truth, the disciples proved themselves to be among God's elect. Of the Twelve, only Judas Iscariot was not chosen, betraying the Lord "so that the Scripture would be fulfilled" (John 17:12; cf. 13:21–30).

BECAUSE THEY WERE GIVEN TO HIM FROM THE FATHER

"I ask on their behalf, I do not ask on behalf of the world, but of those whom You have given Me; for they are Yours; and all things that are Mine are Yours, and Yours are Mine; and I have been glorified in them." (17:9–10)

Because they had responded with belief, and demonstrated the genuineness of that faith through their continued obedience, the disciples showed evidence of what Jesus had always known to be true of them and said earlier—that they had been chosen out of the world by the Father as a gift for Him. This then provides the second and ultimate reason why Jesus was confident that the Father would grant His prayer for the disciples; the Father would be sure to protect and purify them because they were His gift to His Son (cf. vv. 11, 15, 17). By reiterating that He was asking exclusively on **behalf** of **those whom** the Father had **given** Him, Jesus made it clear that He did **not ask on behalf of the world.** Rather, He was asking on behalf of His own who remained in the world after He had left (vv. 11–12).

It is true that God shows a kind of love to all people in the world (what theologians call common grace), even to those who reject the gospel (cf. Mark

10:21). He pleads with sinners to repent (Ezek 18:23, 32; Acts 17:30), extends the gospel invitation to them (Isa 55:1; cf. Matt 11:28–30), "causes His sun to rise on the evil and the good, and sends rain on the righteous and the unrighteous" (Matt 5:45; cf. Ps 145:9; Acts 14:17). But Christ's intercessory work as High Priest is only for those who belong eternally to Him because they have been given by the Father. In fact, the only recorded instance in the New Testament of Christ praying for the unregenerate is His cry from the cross, "Father, forgive them; for they do not know what they are doing" (Luke 23:34). That prayer is a model for believers, who are to "love [their] enemies and pray for those who persecute [them]" (Matt 5:44; 2 Tim 2:26). But the unredeemed world was not His interest in this prayer. His attention was on those whom the Father had given to Him and for whom He was about to die to provide atonement—that they would be protected from the world especially during the immediate events surrounding His arrest, trial, and crucifixion.

Jesus' statement **they are Yours; and all things that are Mine are Yours, and Yours are Mine** underscored His confidence in the fact that the eleven belonged to God. Like the disciples, all believers belong to the Father, having been adopted into His family through the Son (cf. Rom 8:14–17; Gal 3:26; 4:5–7) and sealed and cleansed by the Holy Spirit (Eph 1:13–14; 4:30; Titus 3:5). "Do you not know," Paul wrote to the

Corinthians, "that your body is a temple of the Holy Spirit who is in you, whom you have from God, and that you are not your own? For you have been bought with a price: therefore glorify God in your body" (1 Cor 6:19–20; cf. 7:23). Christians are God's chosen ones (Matt 22:14; John 13:18; Col 3:12; 2 Thess 2:13; 2 Tim 2:10; Titus 1:1; 1 Pet 1:1–2; 2:9), His children (John 1:12; Eph 5:1; Phil 2:15; 1 Pet 1:14; 1 John 3:1–2), His subjects (Luke 6:20; John 3:3, 5; Acts 14:22; Col 1:13; 1 Thess 2:12), His slaves (Acts 4:29; Rom 1:1; 1 Cor 7:22; Phil 1:1; Col 4:12; 2 Tim 2:24; 1 Pet 2:16), and His sheep (Ps 100:3; John 10:7–16, 26–28; 1 Pet 5:2–4).

Christ's statement **all things that are ... Yours are Mine** is nothing less than a claim to deity and full equality with the Father. It again emphasized the intimate unity that the Son shares with the Father (vv. 3, 6–7, 21, 23–24, 26; cf. 16:15). For a mere creature to claim that **all things** of God's were his would be blasphemous presumption. Only one who is Himself God could legitimately claim to be the owner of and ruler over all things. Martin Luther grasped the significance of this claim:

> Everyone may say this, that all we have is God's. But this is much greater, that he turns it around and says, all that is thine is mine. This no creature is able to say before God.... The word: all that is thine is mine, leaves nothing whatever excluded. Are

> all things his, then the eternal deity is also his; otherwise he could not and dared not use the word at all. (Cited in R. C. H. Lenski, *The Interpretation of St. John's Gospel* [Minneapolis: Augsburg, 1943], 1133–34.)

Since the Father and the Son have **all things** in common, believers also belong to Christ (1 Cor 3:23; 15:23; 2 Cor 10:7; Gal 3:29; 5:24). Those who belong to the Father belong to the Son, and vice versa.

The Lord further noted that He had been **glorified in them.** Even now, their faith in Him as the Son of God brought Him glory. Here then Christ gives testimony that the gift of faith given to the disciples enabled them to recognize and to confess Him even in His state of self-humiliation. After His ascension, Christ's glory would continue to be displayed on earth through His followers, even in His absence. That request was in perfect harmony with the Father's purpose—to give the Son a redeemed humanity who would glorify Him forever.

The supreme goal of everything a Christian does is to bring God glory. Paul exhorted the Corinthians, "Whether, then, you eat or drink or whatever you do, do all to the glory of God" (1 Cor 10:31). In his second letter to them, he added, "Therefore we also have as our ambition, whether at home [on earth] or absent [in heaven], to be pleasing to Him" (2 Cor 5:9; cf. Rom 14:7–8). Jesus commanded His followers, "Let your light shine before men in such a way that they may see your good works, and glorify your Father who is in heaven" (Matt 5:16; cf. Phil 2:15). Believers are to reflect Christ's glory in a world of darkness. Paul made that glorious truth crystal clear when he wrote, "God, who said, 'Light shall shine out of darkness,' is the One who has shone in our hearts to give the Light of the knowledge of the glory of God in the face of Christ. But we have this treasure in earthen vessels, so that the surpassing greatness of the power will be of God and not from ourselves" (2 Cor 4:6–7). The desire to glorify Christ will continue into all of eternity, as believers join with angels in magnifying and exalting the Son forever (cf. Rev 4:8–11; 5:11–14; 19:6; 22:3–4).

That the disciples (and all other believers) could be changed from rebellious lovers of this world into sanctified worshipers and glorifiers of God is the miracle of God's grace in salvation. Though regeneration takes place at a moment in time, it is a miracle that was planned in eternity past and that has unending implications for eternity future. All believers (including the eleven disciples) were chosen and claimed by the Father before the world began and promised to the Son as a tangible expression of His infinite love. That is the divine side of salvation. The human side is persevering faith and obedience, by which the disciples had demonstrated that they truly belonged to God.

Believers at all times can be likewise assured that they are truly saved. Objectively, that assurance comes from the Bible's promise that anyone who sincerely embraces Jesus Christ as Lord and Savior will be saved (Rom 10:9–10). Subjectively, that confidence stems from the fruit of enduring faith and continuing obedience in a person's life no matter what the temptation or test. Hear the powerful words of Peter:

> Blessed be the God and Father of our Lord Jesus Christ, who according to His great mercy has caused us to be born again to a living hope through the resurrection of Jesus Christ from the dead, to obtain an inheritance which is imperishable and undefiled and will not fade away, reserved in heaven for you, who are protected by the power of God through faith for a salvation ready to be revealed in the last time. In this you greatly rejoice, even though now for a little while, if necessary, you have been distressed by various trials, so that the proof of your faith, being more precious than gold which is perishable, even though tested by fire, may be found to result in praise and glory and honor at the revelation of Jesus Christ; and though you have not seen Him, you love Him, and though you do not see Him now, but believe in Him, you greatly rejoice with joy inexpressible and full of glory, obtaining as the outcome of your faith the salvation of your souls. (1 Pet 1:3–9; cf. John 10:27; 15:10, 14; 1 John 3:21–24; 4:20; 5:4; cf. Rev 14:12)

Like the eleven, all true disciples of Christ abide in His Word (John 8:31) and lovingly obey His commands

(John 14:15). Such behavior is only possible because their hearts have been changed by God, who has drawn them to the Son (John 6:44) and regenerated them through the Spirit (Titus 3:5). Thus the apostle John could write,

> By this we know that we have come to know Him, if we keep His commandments. The one who says, "I have come to know Him," and does not keep His commandments, is a liar, and the truth is not in him; but whoever keeps His word, in him the love of God has truly been perfected. By this we know that we are in Him: the one who says he abides in Him ought himself to walk in the same manner as He walked. (1 John 2:3–6)

Ensuring the preservation of the disciples' faith is a divine work that the Lord does by His power (cf. John 6:37–40). Nothing can separate His own from His love (Rom 8:31–39), and He is willing and "able also to save forever those who draw near to God through Him, since He always lives to make intercession for them" (Heb 7:25).

In the face of His absence in sin-bearing, though only for a few hours, Jesus proceeded to ask the Father to take up the protection of those whom He had given to Him. Yet, in making that request, Jesus expressed absolute certainty that the Father would do what He asked. His confidence was not in the disciples' steadfastness or ingenuity, but in the love and power of His Father (cf. John 10:28–30). He knew that what the Father had promised in eternity past, He would certainly accomplish and ensure in the present.

04

JESUS PRAYS FOR HIS DISCIPLES—PART 2: AS THOSE WHOM HE IS ABOUT TO LEAVE

JOHN 17:11–19

"I am no longer in the world; and yet they themselves are in the world, and I come to You. Holy Father, keep them in Your name, the name which You have given Me, that they may be one even as We are. While I was with them, I was keeping them in Your name which You have given Me; and I guarded them and not one of them perished but the son of perdition, so that the Scripture would be fulfilled. But now I come to You; and these things I speak in the world so that they may have My joy made full in themselves. I have given them Your word; and the world has hated them, because they are not of the world, even as I am not of the world. I do not ask You to take them out of the world, but to keep them from the evil one. They are not of the world, even as I am not of the world. Sanctify them in the truth; Your word is truth. As You sent Me into the world, I also have sent them into the world. For their sakes I sanctify Myself, that they themselves also may be sanctified in truth." (17:11–19)

Through Jesus Christ, every believer has been granted direct access to the very throne room of God. Each can "draw near with confidence to the throne of grace [and] receive mercy and find grace to help in time of need" (Heb 4:16). Though formerly His enemies, they have been reconciled to God

(2 Cor 5:17–18), having been adopted into His family "through faith in Jesus Christ" (Gal 3:26; cf. 4:5–6; Rom 8:15–17). Because they are His children, the glorious God of the universe graciously, willingly, and lovingly responds to their prayers, no matter how small or feeble they may seem (cf. the exposition of 16:26–27 in chapter 20 of *John 12–21*, The MacArthur New Testament Commentary).

In addition to personal prayers, believers also have the prayers of others, who intercede on their behalf. The apostle Paul emphasized the need for that kind of intercession in the closing paragraphs of his epistle to the Ephesians:

> With all prayer and petition pray at all times in the Spirit, and with this in view, be on the alert with all perseverance and petition for all the saints, and pray on my behalf, that utterance may be given to me in the opening of my mouth, to make known with boldness the mystery of the gospel, for which I am an ambassador in chains; that in proclaiming it I may speak boldly, as I ought to speak. (Eph 6:18–20)

Having just warned his readers about the reality of spiritual warfare (Eph 6:10–17), Paul stressed the critical importance of making supplication "for all the saints" (v. 18). "Pray for us" is a recurring theme throughout his letters (1 Thess 5:25; 2 Thess 3:1; Heb 13:18; cf. Col 4:2–3; 1 Tim 2:7–8). Like Paul, the venerable Spurgeon acutely understood the importance of intercessory prayer. He addressed his congregation with these dramatic words:

> Oh! may God help me, if you cease to pray for me! Let me know the day, and I must cease to preach. Let me know when you intend to cease your prayers, and I shall cry, "O my God, give me this day my tomb, and let me slumber in the dust." (Charles Spurgeon, "Prayer—the Forerunner of Mercy," in *The New Park Street Pulpit* [Pasadena, TX: Pilgrim, 1981], 3:255–56)

The intercession of Christians for each other is an essential element of the church's spiritual life, and the New Testament contains numerous examples of it (e.g., Acts 12:5; 20:36; 21:5; 2 Cor 1:11; 9:14; Eph 1:16; 6:18–19; Phil 1:4; Col 4:12).

But other Christians are not the only ones who intercede on behalf of the believer. The Holy "Spirit also helps our weakness; for we do not know how to pray as we should, but the Spirit Himself intercedes for us with groanings too deep for words" (Rom 8:26). The skewed perspectives, human imperfections, and spiritual limitations that plague Christians in this life keep them from praying as they ought to pray—in absolute consistency with God's will. But the indwelling Spirit intercedes on behalf of each Christian, faithfully bringing his needs before God even when he is confused as to what those needs truly are. The Spirit's prayers are always answered "because He intercedes for the saints according to the will of God" (v. 27).

Yet, beyond all of that, there is another who prays for believers—none other than the Lord Jesus Christ, who is "seated at the right hand of God" (Col 3:1) and "always lives to make intercession for [His people]" (Heb 7:25). Like the Spirit, the blessed Christ intercedes continually for His own, often in response to the accusations of Satan (1 John 2:1; Rev 12:10), and always in accord with the will of God. His mediatorial work of intercession is as real and indispensable as His work of atonement. It was the death of the Lord Jesus Christ that gave believers eternal life; it is His intercessory work for them that sustains that life, bringing them from justification, through sanctification, to glorification (cf. Rom 8:30). His intercession is the guarantee that undergirds Christ's promise, "All that the Father gives Me will come to Me, and the one who comes to Me I will certainly not cast out.... For this is the will of My Father, that everyone who beholds the Son and believes in Him will have eternal life, and I Myself will raise him up on the last day" (John 6:37, 40).

Christ's prayer in this chapter provides a priceless preview of His current intercessory work, which did not formally begin until after His ascension. In entrusting His followers to His Father, interceding on their behalf just a few hours before the cross, Jesus vividly displayed the profound depths of both His communion with God and His compassion for

His own. As one commentator observes, the sublime magnificence of this aspect of the prayer

> surpasses all literature in its setting forth the identity of being and power and love in the twofold personality of the God-Man. We are brought by it to the mercy-seat, into the heaven of heavens, to the very heart of God; and we find there a presentation of the most mysterious and incomprehensible love to the human race, embodied in the Person, enshrined in the words, of the only begotten Son. (H. R. Reynolds, *St. John*, The Pulpit Commentary, ed. H. D. M. Spence and Joseph S. Exell [Grand Rapids: Eerdmans, 1981], 17:340)

This petition marks the transition from His earthly to His heavenly ministry. After completing His work of redemption on the cross and triumphing over sin, death, and the forces of hell, Jesus ascended to heaven. There, He continually "intercedes for us" (Rom 8:34) while seated "at the right hand of God" (Col 3:1; Heb 10:12; 1 Pet 3:22; cf. Matt 22:44; 26:64; Acts 2:33–34; 5:31; 7:55–56; Eph 1:20; Heb 1:3; 8:1; 12:2).

The prayer itself has been divided into three sections. In the first section (vv. 1–5) Jesus prayed for His glory; in the last section (vv. 20–26) He prayed for all believers. But between those first and last sections, the Lord prayed specifically for the eleven disciples—as those whom the Father had given Him (vv. 6–10), and as those whom He was about to leave (vv. 11–19).

All twelve disciples had been present in the upper room when Jesus humbly washed their feet (13:5), and when they ate a final meal together (13:12). But not all twelve were true disciples (cf. 6:66; 8:31). One of them, Judas the son of Simon Iscariot, was a traitor (13:21)—a characteristic that he had hidden from everyone else except Christ (13:11). In fact, when Jesus mentioned that someone would betray Him, none of the other disciples even suspected Judas (13:22). After exposing Judas as the betrayer, He said to him, "What you do, do quickly" (13:27). But even then, the other disciples did not know "for what purpose He had said this to him. For some were supposing because Judas had the money box, that Jesus was saying to him, 'Buy the things we have need of for the feast'; or else, that he should give something to the poor" (13:28–29).

With Judas gone, only the eleven remained. (After the events of the resurrection and ascension, Matthias would be chosen as Judas's replacement [Acts 1:26].) It was to them that Jesus spoke the profound words of the upper room discourse (in chapters 14–16). And it was for them that Jesus specifically prayed in verses 6–19.

A quick survey of the behavior of those eleven men underscores the necessity of Jesus' prayer on their behalf. First among the apostles was Peter (Matt 10:2–4; Mark 3:16–19; Luke 6:14–16; Acts 1:13), whose characteristic outspokenness (cf. Matt 16:21–23) had earned him a dire rebuke from the Lord earlier that evening. After impetuously promising that he would die for Jesus, he heard this chilling reply: "Will you lay down your life for Me? Truly, truly, I say to you, a rooster will not crow until you deny Me three times" (John 13:38). Peter, who had been concerned about who would betray his Master (13:24), must have been profoundly distraught by the Lord's prediction about him. This, compounded by the realization that Jesus was going away, surely weighed heavy on his heart as he heard the Lord's intercession on his behalf.

The other disciples were similarly distraught at the thought of Christ's absence. Their own weakness and seeming lack of readiness would have been an inescapable concern. None of them appear particularly savvy or resourceful. They were not highly educated (Acts 4:13), nor did they have much in the way of material resources, since they had given up everything to follow Jesus (Mark 10:28). Many of the disciples were common fishermen (Peter, Andrew, James, and John were for sure [cf. Matt 4:18–21], and possibly Thomas, Philip, and Nathanael [Bartholomew] were as well [cf. John 21:2–3]). Others came from even less prestigious backgrounds. Matthew had been a tax collector (Matt 9:9) and was thereby despised by the Jews; while Simon had been a political revolutionary (as his name "the Zealot" indicates; Luke 6:15; Acts 1:13), and was thereby despised by the Romans.

They were ordinary men, with ordinary weaknesses. Peter was impetuous (as noted above); Thomas was a skeptic (John 20:25); and James and John were hotheaded "sons of thunder" (Mark 3:17; cf. Mark 9:38; Luke 9:52–54). Like Philip (John 6:5–7; 14:8), the rest lacked spiritual perception. Like Thaddeus (cf. John 14:22), they all failed to understand Christ's role in His first coming (as the Suffering Servant). Like the sons of Zebedee (Matt 20:21–22), they all evidenced pride and a desire to hold a preeminent position (Matt 20:24). And like Peter (John 13:38), whose name meant "rock" (Matt 16:18), they all became cowards when the Lord was arrested (John 16:32). In fact, their spiritual resolve was such that when they were supposed to be praying, at the moment of Christ's supreme agony (Luke 22:44), Jesus found them sleeping (v. 46).

From a human perspective, this ragamuffin group of followers was anything but extraordinary or impressive (cf. 1 Cor 1:16–31). Yet they were called to continue Jesus' work in the world after He was gone—having been given the responsibility of taking the gospel throughout the world (Matt 28:18–20; cf. Acts 1:8), and shepherding the church through their teaching and oversight (cf. Acts 2:42; 6:4). They played a vital role in the future of the Christian faith, because God had chosen them to tell the world of redemption through His Son (cf. Eph 2:20).

It is no wonder, then, that Jesus interceded for them, and that the bulk of His prayer concentrates on these eleven men. His confidence was not in their resolve or resourcefulness (of which they had little), but in the power and love of His Father. Jesus knew that the Father would hear and answer His prayers, not because the eleven were inherently capable, but because they were part of those whom the Father had promised Him from before the foundation of the world. The striking reality of prayer is that it is not designed to change God's will, but to call for its fulfillment. Furthermore, the Lord purposely prayed aloud so that His disciples could hear Him and be strengthened and encouraged.

Soon Jesus would **no longer** be **in the world** to protect and care for His disciples, although **they themselves** would remain **in the world.** His use of the present tense is indicative of the fact that, after the events of the next few hours transpired, His earthly mission would be completed. The time was no longer future, it had arrived. He was going away but they were staying behind. Though they surely wished to go with Him (cf. 14:1–6), it was critical that, for the time being, they remain and take the gospel to the world (cf. Matt 28:18–20; John 17:18; Acts 1:7–8). Since in the plan of God there would have been no church, and no subsequent generations of believers, if the disciples had not been left as witnesses to the gospel, this intercession on their behalf is weighty. It is a means God used for activating His will.

And the **world,** where the disciples would remain, was certain to be hostile to them. It was, after all, a place of hateful rebellion against God and against His Son (John 1:11; 7:7; 15:18–19; 16:33; cf. Luke 21:12–19). Once Jesus left, antagonism toward Him (under the direction of Satan—cf. John 14:30; 16:11) would be redirected toward the disciples. They were therefore in desperate need of the Father's protection from the world around them. The world, in spiritual darkness and confusion (John 1:5; 3:19; 8:12; 9:39; 12:46), gave residence to sins and temptations of every kind—from the "doctrines of demons" (1 Tim 4:1) to the abominable acts of the heathen that were too disgraceful even to mention (cf. Eph 5:12). Thus, as they went forth to proclaim the gospel, the disciples also needed the Father's sanctifying, purifying power and grace.

Having established the reasons why He knew the Father would answer His prayer (in vv. 6–10), Jesus now made those two requests on behalf of His disciples: that they would receive spiritual protection (in vv. 11b–16) and sanctifying purity (in vv. 17–19) from the Father.

THE REQUEST FOR SPIRITUAL PROTECTION

"Holy Father, keep them in Your name, the name which You have given Me, that they may be one even as We are. While I was with them, I was keeping them in Your name which You have given Me; and I guarded them and not one of them perished but the son of perdition, so that the Scripture would be fulfilled. But now I come to You; and these things I speak in the world so that they may have My joy made full in themselves. I have given them Your word; and the world has hated them, because they are not of the world, even as I am not of the world. I do not ask You to take them out of the world, but to keep them from the evil one. They are not of the world, even as I am not of the world." (17:11*b*–16)

Jesus began the requests for His disciples by addressing God as **Holy Father** (a title for God found only here). The emphasis on God's holiness sets the stage for the rest of this section (in vv. 11–19), which targets the holiness of the disciples in the midst of the hostile and wicked world. Their relationship to God was a sanctifying one. They were unholy men, but through the Son they had been brought into a purifying relationship with Holy God.

Jesus' first petition, **keep them** (which is reiterated in v. 15), is a request for the disciples' spiritual security. God's **name** represents all that He is, though in this case there is a marked emphasis on His holiness (since Jesus just referred to Him as "Holy Father"). Jesus asked the Father to guard the disciples according to His holy character and attributes. That request is all-encompassing, and extends to all believers, as A. C. Gaebelein explains:

> That keeping means everything. Keeping from falling away, from evil doctrines, from being overcome by sorrow, or in tribulation and suffering, keeping them in life and in death. From this first petition of our Lord's prayer we learn the absolute security of a true believer. If a true believer, one who belongs to Christ, who has been given by the Father to the Son, for whom the Son of God intercedes, can be lost, it would mean the loss of Christ's glory, the loss of a part of the travail of His soul. (*The Gospel of John* [Wheaton: Van Kampen, 1936], 320)

The Lord again emphasized His perfect oneness with the Father by noting that the name of the Father is also **the name which** the Father has **given** the Son. God's holy character was reflected perfectly in Him. "No one has seen God at any time," John wrote earlier in his gospel. "[But] the only begotten God who is in the bosom of the Father, He has explained Him" (John 1:18). Jesus had provided the disciples with a perfect picture of who God is and what He expects.

The Father's protection was essential for the disciples for at least two reasons. First, it secured their glorification, as it does for all believers. Christians "are protected by the power of God through faith for a salvation ready to be revealed in the last time" (1 Pet 1:5). Romans 8:29–30 reveals that God's providential care forges an unbroken chain leading from eternity past to eternity future: "For those whom He foreknew, He also predestined to become conformed to the image of His Son, so that He would be the firstborn among many brethren; and these whom He predestined, He also called; and these whom He called, He also justified; and these whom He justified, He also glorified."

Second, the Father's protection also secured their unity with one another—**that they** would **be one even as** Christ and the Father **are.** That unity the Lord had in mind is the spiritual unity that all believers possess, namely, the life of God in their regenerated souls, secured to them forever by His power and presence. The emphasis here is not on a fluctuating, visible unity in the church, but on the real, constant unity that is invisible. The Lord is praying for the essential oneness of believers that they share in common eternal life. This prayer is answered every time a sinner is regenerated.

The unity of invisible eternal life implanted in Christ's followers is the foundation for a visible unity that crosses all organizational lines and that produces an effective gospel and testimony to the lost (cf. the exposition of 13:35 in chapter 8 of *John 12–21*, The MacArthur New Testament Commentary). It is produced by the Holy Spirit (Eph 4:3), who indwells every believer (Rom 8:9). Practically, this spiritual unity of divine life produces a common love for the Lord (1 John 4:19–21), commitment to His Word (Eph 4:13), affection for His people (Col 3:14), and separation from all that is ungodly and worldly (1 John 2:15–17).

During His earthly ministry, Jesus had been **keeping them in** the Father's **name which** He had **given** Him. In fact, He **guarded** the disciples so well that **not one of them perished but the son of perdition.** The Lord had taught them, empowered them, and shielded them from the attacks of the hostile Jewish authorities (cf. Matt 12:2–8; 15:2–9). Soon, in Gethsemane, He would do so again (John 18:4–9). Jesus used two different Greek words for "keeping" (*tēreō*) and "guarded" (*phulassō*). The first speaks of protection by means of restraint, and carries the idea of preserving or watching over. It is often used in John's gospel to refer to keeping God's words or commandments. The second refers to protection from outside dangers. It is an act of safeguarding, used in Luke to picture the strong man who guards his house (Luke 11:21). Taken together, the words give a picture of complete deliverance from all perils, and lasting security. The Son asks the Father to secure His disciples, knowing that it is the Father's will (John 6:39). The omniscient Son always prayed in perfect agreement with His Father (John 5:30). The work of securing His people is a Trinitarian work. In John 5:17–19 Jesus

> answered [His Jewish opponents], "My Father is working until now, and I Myself am working." For this reason therefore the Jews were seeking all the more to kill Him, because He not only was breaking the Sabbath, but also was calling God His own Father, making Himself equal with God. Therefore Jesus answered and was saying to them, "Truly, truly, I say to you, the Son can do nothing of Himself, unless it is something He sees the Father doing; for whatever the Father does, these things the Son also does in like manner."

In Ephesians 1:13–14 Paul wrote,

> In Him [Christ], you also, after listening to the message of truth, the gospel of your salvation—having also believed, you were sealed in Him with the Holy Spirit of promise, who is given as a pledge of our inheritance, with a view to the redemption of God's own possession, to the praise of His glory.

The loss of Judas, **the son of perdition,** was not due to Jesus failing to keep him. He knew all along that he was a false disciple (6:70–71). Far from catching Jesus by surprise, Judas's apostasy took place **so that the Scripture would be fulfilled** (see the discussion of 13:18 in chapter 7 of *John 12–21,* The MacArthur New Testament Commentary; cf. Pss 41:9; 109:8; Acts 1:20). Judas, of course, was still personally responsible for his wicked actions (cf. Matt 26:24 and Mark 14:21). As Leon Morris rightly notes:

> The reference to the fulfilling of Scripture brings out the divine purpose. This does not mean that Judas was an automaton. He was a responsible person and acted freely. But God used that man's evil act to bring about his own purpose. There is a combination of the human and the divine, but in this passage it is the divine aspect rather than the human that receives stress. In the end God's will was done in the handing over of Jesus to be crucified. (Leon Morris, *The Gospel According to John*, The New International Commentary on the New Testament [Grand Rapids: Eerdmans, 1995], 645)

(For further discussion of the interplay between human responsibility and divine sovereignty, see the introduction to the previous chapter of this volume.) Yet, what Judas (and Satan—John 13:27) intended for evil, God in His perfect purposes worked together for good (cf. Gen 50:20; Rom 9:17). God would use the most horrific event in human history—the murder of His Son—as the means by which He would atone for the sins of His elect.

The prophetic Scriptures fulfilled in Jesus were certainly much broader than just those that reference Judas. The Old Testament foretold that the Christ would be a descendant of Abraham (Gen 22:18), from the tribe of Judah (Gen 49:10), of the family of Jesse (Isa 11:1), in the line of David (Jer 23:5). He would be born in Bethlehem (Mic 5:2), have a forerunner (Isa 40:3; Mal 3:1), begin His ministry in Galilee (Isa 9:1; cf. Matt 4:12–17), be anointed by the Spirit (Isa 11:2; cf. Matt 3:16–17), have a ministry of miracles (Isa 35:5–6; cf. Matt 9:35), and bring healing and life to His people (Isa 61:1–2; cf. Luke 4:18). At the end of His ministry, He would enter Jerusalem on a donkey (Zech 9:9; Luke 19:35–37). Then, having been fully rejected by the Jewish leaders (Ps 118:22; cf. 1 Pet 2:7), He would be falsely accused (Isa 53:7; Matt 27:12), made to suffer (Isa 53:5–6; cf. Matt 26:67), and crucified with thieves (Isa 53:12; cf. Matt 27:38). Moreover, His garments would be divided (Ps 22:18; cf. John 19:23–24), His side pierced (Zech 12:10; cf. John 19:34), and His body buried in a rich man's tomb (Isa 53:9; cf. Matt 27:57ff.). All of this took place just as it had been foretold by the Old Testament.

Hence, after His resurrection, Jesus could rebuke two of His followers on the road to Emmaus for not understanding that the Old Testament Scriptures revealed the necessity of His suffering and death (Luke 24:25–26). As Luke records, "Then beginning with Moses and with all the prophets, He explained to them the things concerning Himself in all the Scriptures" (v. 27). Jesus knew that Judas's betrayal had been part of the divine plan all along. Judas did not defect because Jesus failed to protect him. Rather, Judas fell because he had never been a true disciple of Christ in the first place and was void of spiritual life; and because his role in Jesus' death was part of God's sovereignly predetermined plan.

Confident of the Father's protective care for the disciples, the Lord looked to His return to the Father. **But now I come to You,** Jesus acknowledged, **and these things I speak in the world so that they may have My joy made full in themselves.** For the third time that evening, Jesus spoke of the joy that was His legacy to His followers (cf. 15:11; 16:20–24). Understanding the Father's protection (cf. Rom 8:33–39) and Christ's intercession inevitably produced joy in the hearts of the listening disciples. This had to have been a stunningly wonderful experience for the disciples—to hear their Lord praying as He did for them to the Father to guarantee their eternal glory and remove all fear that they might fail and perish. Elsewhere, Jesus had earlier prayed that the disciples would share in the fullness of His life (John 10:10; 11:25–26) and in His peace (14:27); now He prayed for their fullness of joy. All of this concern and care for His own is enriching because it reveals His love for them (John 13:1; Rom 8:35–39).

The Lord's use of the personal possessive pronoun, **My,** indicates that this was not just any kind of arbitrary happiness. It was His joy—both that which was based in Him, and which He Himself experienced. It was the joy that was "set before Him" (Heb 12:2); joy that was not founded on immediate circumstances but on the eternal purposes of God. It was joy that came not from momentary happiness, but from the knowing that the Father was pleased with His perfect obedience (cf. 2 Cor 4:17–18). The disciples would share in that joy by experiencing the eternal life that Jesus made possible through His death (cf. 16:22; 17:3, 18). All believers, in the generations that have followed the eleven, have shared in that same joy.

Having spoken only divine truth, Jesus had **given them** God's **word,** which the world rejected (5:38). In the past, God had spoken through His prophets; but now He had spoken through His Son (Heb 1:1–2; cf. John 1:1, 18). Yet, just as the world had rejected the message of the prophets beforehand, so it also rejected the message of the Son (cf. Mark 6:1–12). As John had earlier written about Jesus, "He came to His own, and those who were His own did not receive Him" (John 1:11). The Lord Himself rebuked His opponents with these words, "The Father who sent Me, He has testified of Me. You have neither heard His voice at any time nor seen His form. You do not have His word abiding in you, for you do not believe Him whom He sent" (John 5:37–38). And later, "If you believed Moses, you would believe Me, for he wrote about Me. But if you do not believe his writings, how will you believe My words?" (5:46–47).

In contrast to the world, which rejected the message of Christ, the disciples had received and believed His word (John 17:8). Because of that, the world **hated them,** just as it had hated Jesus. After all, **they** were **not of the world, even as** Jesus was **not of the world** (8:23). Because the disciples had been born again from above (3:3, 5), their citizenship was no longer in the world but in heaven (Phil 3:20)—making them aliens and strangers on this earth (cf. 1 Pet 1:1; 2:11).

Though they were not part of the world, Christ did not request that they be removed from the world. He plainly said to the Father, **I do not ask You to take them out of the world.** Jesus' earlier promise to them was not that they would be taken out of the world, but that in Him they would triumph over it (cf. 16:33). Like the disciples, true believers today are in the world, without being part of its evil system. James declared forcefully, "You adulteresses, do you not know that friendship with the world is hostility toward God? Therefore whoever wishes to be a friend of the world makes himself an enemy of God" (Jas 4:4; cf. 1:27). The apostle John commanded believers, "Do not love the world nor the things in the world. If anyone loves the world, the love of the Father is not in him" (1 John 2:15).

Paul explained to the Corinthians that he "did not at all mean [that they should not associate] with the immoral people of this world, or with the covetous and swindlers, or with idolaters, for then you would have to go out of the world" (1 Cor 5:10). On the contrary, believers are to reach the lost world with the truth of the gospel (cf. Matt 5:13–16). That is their primary reason for remaining here; it is the one thing they could not do better in heaven. The glorious truth is that "whoever will call on the name of the Lord will be saved" (Rom 10:13). But as Paul goes on to ask, "How then will they call on Him in whom they have not believed? How will they believe in Him whom they have not heard? And how will they hear without a preacher?" (v. 14). Far from taking believers out of the world, God "has committed to us the word of reconciliation. Therefore, we are ambassadors for Christ" (2 Cor 5:19–20).

Though He does not ask for them to be removed from the world, He does reiterate the basic request of verse 11, that while they live on the earth the Father would **keep them from the evil one.** There is nothing that Satan (the prince of this world—Eph 2:2) would like better than to destroy saving faith; to snatch a soul from the safety of Christ's and the Father's hands (10:28–29) would be his desire. He tried to destroy Job's faith, but after all the calamities that Satan brought upon him, Job's response showed that the faith God gives cannot be destroyed. It is by divine power an enduring faith:

> Then Job answered the Lord and said, "I know that You can do all things, and that no purpose of Yours can be thwarted. 'Who is this that hides counsel without knowledge?' Therefore I have declared that which I did not understand, things too

> wonderful for me, which I did not know. 'Hear, now, and I will speak; I will ask You, and You instruct me.' I have heard of You by the hearing of the ear; but now my eye sees You; therefore I retract, and I repent in dust and ashes." (Job 42:1–6)

Satan also sought to destroy Peter's faith. Jesus warned him, "Simon, Simon, behold, Satan has demanded permission to sift you like wheat; but I have prayed for you, that your faith may not fail; and you, when once you have turned again, strengthen your brothers" (Luke 22:31–32). It is true that Peter failed miserably when he denied the Lord, but his faith endured. He repented (cf. Matt 26:75), Jesus restored him (John 21:15–19), and he was the powerful evangelist for Christ in the early church (Acts 2–12). The Lord's intercession for His people guarantees that none of them will be reclaimed by Satan.

As He concluded His first request for the disciples, Jesus reiterated the fact that **they are not of the world, even as** He is **not of the world.** On the one hand, that meant they would face the persecution of the world—for they would be treated by unbelievers just as Christ Himself was treated. Yet, on the other hand, it also meant they would enjoy the protection of the Father, for they would likewise be treated by the Father in the same manner as Christ. Verse 16 is therefore more than just a restatement of verse 14. It is a reiteration by the Son, before the Father, of the solidarity that those whom He was leaving in the world shared with Him.

THE REQUEST FOR SANCTIFYING PURITY

"Sanctify them in the truth; Your word is truth. As You sent Me into the world, I also have sent them into the world. For their sakes I sanctify Myself, that they themselves also may be sanctified in truth." (17:17–19)

Having prayed for their spiritual protection from the world, Jesus continued by asking the Father to sanctify and purify the disciples as they prepared to preach the truth to the world. It was not enough that they be safeguarded from outside evils. They must also be internally conformed more and more to the Son. Though they had already been cleansed (referring to salvation—John 15:3), they still needed to occasionally have their feet washed from the filth of this world (John 13:10; cf. Heb 12:1–2; 1 John 2:1–2). The Evil One would aggressively try to derail this work of sanctification, but the Father Himself guaranteed it through the Word of truth (v. 17), empowered by the Spirit of truth (14:17; 15:26; 16:13).

Jesus therefore asked His Father to **sanctify them in the truth,** to set them apart from sin. The instrument of sanctification is God's revealed, inscripturated **word,** contained in Old and New Testaments, the totality of which **is truth.** God's Word and truth are synonymous.

> "Thine own word is truth" certifies the inerrancy and infallibility of the Word excepting no portion of it. The holy garment of the Word is seamless; it has no rents of error—or call them mistakes—which hands today must sew up. "Thine own word" signifies all of it, the Word of the Old Testament on which Jesus placed his approval again and again, plus the revelation that Jesus added in person with the promise of its perfect preservation through the Paraclete (14:26; 16:13). (R. C. H. Lenski, *The Interpretation of St. John's Gospel* [Minneapolis: Augsburg, 1943], 1149)

Throughout His ministry, Jesus put a premium on the written Word of God. He saw the Old Testament Scriptures as the "word of God" (cf. Matt 15:6; 22:31), and repeatedly affirmed their inerrancy (Matt 5:18; John 10:35) and historical accuracy (cf. Jesus' testimony to the historicity of various Old Testament characters such as Jonah [Matt 12:40]; Noah [Matt 24:38]; Moses [Mark 12:26]; Abel [Luke 11:51]; Lot [Luke 17:29]; and Lot's wife [Luke 17:32]). As He told the Pharisees, "It is easier for heaven and earth to pass away than for one stroke of a letter of the law to fail" (Luke 16:17). He further saw the Old Testament as being perfectly fulfilled in Him (Matt 5:17; Luke 24:27; John 5:39; 13:18; cf. Acts 13:27), such that those who rejected Him simultaneously rejected the Scriptures (John 5:46–47). During His ministry, Jesus viewed His own words as words from God (John 7:16; 8:26–28, 38; 12:49; 14:10, 24), as He revealed the Father through everything He said and did (John 1:18; 6:69; cf. Heb 1:1–2; 1 John 1:1–3). As He was about to depart, while in the upper room with His disciples, He promised the eleven that through them the rest of His word would be revealed (John 14:26; 15:26–27; 16:12–15). That promise is fulfilled by the New Testament.

Thus, in referring to the **word** that is **truth,** Jesus was speaking not only of His immediate words (as if the red letters in Scripture comprised the only true words), but of the entirety of Scripture. His revelation was in perfect harmony with that of the Old Testament; and His disciples were authorized by Him to record the revelation He would give them through His Spirit. All of it, from Genesis to Revelation, is truth (cf. Pss 19:7; 119:160). And all of it is necessary for the believer's sanctification (cf. Eph 5:26; 2 Tim 3:16–17). As the apostle Peter would instruct the Christians of Asia Minor many years later, "Like newborn babies, long for the pure milk of the word, so that by it you may grow in respect to salvation" (1 Pet 2:2). "Your word I have treasured in my heart," wrote the psalmist, "that I may not sin against You" (Ps 119:11). It is "the word of His grace," Paul told the Ephesian elders, "which is able to build you up and to give you the inheritance among all those who are sanctified" (Acts 20:32).

Only sanctified believers are ready to be **sent into the world** as the Father **sent** Christ **into the**

world. These words, directed at the eleven, served as a preview of the Great Commission the Lord would give these same disciples following His resurrection (Matt 28:18–20; cf. Acts 1:7–8). Having been set apart from the world and transformed by God's grace, the disciples would be the heralds of that same grace to the very world that hated them. In the same way that they were disciples of Jesus, they were to "make disciples" of Christ in "all the nations, baptizing them in the name of the Father and the Son and the Holy Spirit, teaching them to observe all that [Christ] commanded [them]" (Matt 28:19–20). Just as Jesus had been sent to the world by His Father, so now the disciples were being sent to the world by Jesus. Through their witness, the world would be exposed to the gospel and many would come to saving faith.

But no such salvation would even be possible, if it were not for the sacrificial death of the Son. The Lord returned to that thought in verse 19, acknowledging that what He was about to endure at the cross would make salvation possible both for the eleven and for those who would be saved through their extended ministries. **For** the disciples' **sakes** Jesus would **sanctify** Himself; that is, He would set Himself apart to righteously obey the Father's will by dying on the cross. It was only because He atoned for their sins **that they themselves also** would be **sanctified in truth** (cf. Heb 10:10; 13:12). Having been justified through their faith in Him (cf. Rom 5:1, 8), they would be daily conformed more and more into His perfect image (Rom 8:29; cf. Phil 2:12–13; 3:21).

As He always did, Jesus prayed consistently with the will of the Father. He asked the Father to do what He had predetermined in eternity past to do—to pour out His love, grace, mercy, and power on those whom He had chosen and given to Jesus. It is on that basis that Christ appealed to the Father to protect and secure the disciples. Guarded by the Father, interceded for by Christ, and indwelt by the Holy Spirit, these men, along with the apostle Paul (1 Cor 15:8), would provide the solid foundation upon which all believers in the ages to come would rest (Eph 2:20).

05

JESUS PRAYS FOR ALL BELIEVERS—PART 1: THAT THEY WOULD BE PRESENTLY UNITED IN TRUTH

JOHN 17:20–23

"I do not ask on behalf of these alone, but for those also who believe in Me through their word; that they may all be one; even as You, Father, are in Me and I in You, that they also may be in Us, so that the world may believe that You sent Me. The glory which You have given Me I have given to them, that they may be one, just as We are one; I in them and You in Me, that they may be perfected in unity, so that the world may know that You sent Me, and loved them, even as You have loved Me." (17:20–23)

As noted in the previous chapter of this volume, the unity Christ prayed for is not an outward, organizational unity, but the inward, spiritual unity based on believers' life in Christ. Because of their union with Jesus Christ—since "the one who joins himself to the Lord is one spirit with Him" (1 Cor 6:17)—all believers are one with each other as well (Gal 3:28). In the words of the Westminster Confession of Faith, "The catholic or universal Church, which is invisible, consists of the whole number of the elect, that have been, are, or shall be gathered into one, under Christ the head thereof; and is the spouse, the body, the fullness of him that filleth all in all" (25.1).

How does that spiritual unity manifest itself in practice? In Philippians 2:2, Paul listed four marks of the unity that characterizes the true church.

First, unity results in believers "being of the same mind." That does not mean that they share all the same likes and dislikes. Nor does it entail complete agreement on all the secondary doctrinal issues that godly men differ over. Rather, it signifies that true believers are controlled by a deep knowledge of the Word of Christ that is energized in them by the power of the Spirit (cf. Col 3:16). Because they walk in the Spirit, they maintain the same spiritual attitude.

Second, unity results in believers "maintaining the same love"; that is, they love each other equally. That does not mean that they have the same emotional commitment to everyone, which is impossible. The love in view here is *agapē* love, the love not of emotional attraction, but of will and choice. It is expressed when believers are "devoted to one another in brotherly love; [and] give preference to one another in honor" (Rom 12:10). It has been "poured out within our hearts through the Holy Spirit who was given to us" (Rom 5:5).

Third, unity results in believers being "united in spirit." The Greek word literally means "one-souled." It refers to a passionate, common commitment to the same spiritual goals. By definition it excludes such divisive attitudes as personal ambition, selfishness, hatred, envy, jealousy, and the countless other manifestations of the evil fruit of self-love.

Finally, unity results in believers being "intent on one purpose." Because they are of the same mind, love each other, and are united in spirit, they have the same goal—advancing the kingdom of God. But believers can interrupt their spiritual unity by fleshly behavior and need to be exhorted to have "one mind striving together for the faith of the gospel" (Phil 1:27).

But in our obsessively tolerant age, the opposite extreme poses a far more serious threat to true spiritual unity. In the name of love, many work hard to achieve a superficial, false, sinful unity that is broad enough to embrace false Christians and even those who deny the central truths of the Christian faith. Genuine biblical love, however, cannot be divorced from biblical truth (Eph 4:15). Far from compromising it, God's people are called to "contend earnestly for the faith which was once for all handed down to the saints" (Jude 3). The true church of Jesus Christ cannot unite with those who deny the essential truths of the gospel (2 John 7–11), or who affirm a false gospel (Gal 1:6–9). "Do not be bound together with unbelievers," Paul commanded the Corinthians, "for what partnership have righteousness and lawlessness, or what fellowship has light with darkness? Or what harmony has Christ with Belial, or what has a believer in common with an unbeliever?" (2 Cor 6:14–15). True unity is the reality among true Christians.

As He concluded His magnificent High Priestly Prayer, the unity of His followers was very much on the heart of the Lord Jesus Christ. Having prayed for

His glory (vv. 1–5) and for His disciples (vv. 6–19), the Savior expanded His prayer to include all future believers—those who would come to Him through the power of the Word (v. 17), the witness of the disciples (v. 18), and the sacrifice of the cross (v. 19). The Lord made two requests on their behalf: that they would be united in the truth, and that they would be reunited with Him in eternal glory. The first of those requests is the subject of this chapter.

The Lord's first request may be examined under four headings: the root of true unity, the request for true unity, the representation of true unity, and the result of true unity.

THE ROOT OF TRUE UNITY

"I do not ask on behalf of these alone, but for those also who believe in Me through their word ..." (17:20)

The opening words of verse 20 introduce the third thing for which Christ said He was not praying. In verse 9, He made it clear that He was not interceding on behalf of the unbelieving world (see the discussion of this point in chapter 03 of this volume), while in verse 15, He said that He was not asking for the disciples to be removed from the world. His words **I do not ask on behalf of these alone** introduce another group distinct from the then-living disciples for whom He had just prayed (vv. 6–19). Jesus looked ahead through the centuries and prayed for all the believers who were to come in the future. Although the vast majority had not yet been born, they nevertheless were and had been for eternity on the heart of the Savior. He knew them all, since their names have "been written from the foundation of the world in the book of life" (Rev 13:8; cf. 3:5; 17:8; 20:12, 15; 21:27; Phil 4:3). Christ's intercession for us, which began with this prayer 2,000 years ago, continues to this day, "since He always lives to make intercession for [us]" (Heb 7:25).

Jesus further identified these future believers as those who would **believe in** Him (John 1:12; 3:15–16, 36; 6:40, 47; 7:37–38; 11:25–26; 20:31; Acts 13:38–39; 16:31; Rom 10:9–10; Gal 3:22), reminding all again that salvation comes through faith alone, "not as a result of works, so that no one may boast" (Eph 2:9; cf. Rom 3:20–30; Gal 2:16; 3:8, 11–14, 24). The Lord's reference to believing in Him again preserves the biblical balance concerning salvation. On the one hand, only those given by the Father to Christ will come to Him (v. 6; cf. 6:44). But on the other hand, their salvation does not take place apart from personal faith (cf. Rom 10:9–10). In much the same way, the reality that the Lord will draw those whom He chooses to Himself (John 6:44; Acts 2:39; 11:18; 13:48; 16:14) does not obviate the church's responsibility to evangelize the lost (Matt 28:19–20; Luke 24:47; Acts 1:8).

The apostles and their associates were the human authors of the New Testament (John 14:26; 16:13–15; cf. Eph 2:20), therefore all who would be saved in the future would come to Christ **through** their **word.** Some would hear that message directly from the apostles' own preaching (e.g., Acts 2:14–42; 3:11–26; 4:8–12; 5:30–32; 13:14–41; 16:11–14; 17:22–34; 18:4–11). Most, however, would hear the apostolic message through the written Word of their Spirit-inspired writings. The early church was reading the truths of Scripture when reading "the apostles' teaching" (Acts 2:42; cf. Jude 17). Through the centuries all who have preached the true gospel have preached the apostles' word. As Paul wrote in Romans 10:17, "Faith comes from hearing, and hearing by the word of Christ" (lit., "a speech about Christ")—the apostolic message of salvation.

The disciples at that point hardly seemed ready to turn the world upside down (cf. Acts 17:6). One of them, Judas Iscariot, had turned traitor, and was at that moment preparing to lead those who would arrest Jesus to Gethsemane (18:1–3). Their brash, bold, seemingly fearless leader, Peter, would soon cower before the accusations of a servant girl, and repeatedly deny the Lord (John 18:17; cf. vv. 25–27). The rest of the disciples would abandon Jesus after His arrest and flee for their lives (Matt 26:56).

But Christ's prayer ensures that the apostles' ministry would be successful. In His omniscience,

Jesus knew that they would fulfill their role in redemptive history. The gospel would prevail, despite the apostles' weakness, the world's hatred, and Satan's opposition. Empowered by the Holy Spirit (Acts 1:8; 2:1–4), those early disciples would begin the chain of witnesses that continues unbroken down to the present day (cf. 2 Tim 2:2). All of the church's evangelistic success is the result of the Lord's request in verse 20 for those who would believe in the future. This request guaranteed the successful establishment of the church, and the success of its evangelistic ministry from apostolic times to the present. "I will build My church," Jesus declared, "and the gates of Hades will not overpower it" (Matt 16:18).

THE REQUEST FOR TRUE UNITY

"that they may all be one ..." (17:21*a*)

Despite their outward denominational differences, all true Christians are spiritually united by regeneration in their belief that salvation is by grace alone through faith alone, in Christ alone, and their commitment to the absolute authority of Scripture. All those who savingly believe in the Lord Jesus Christ "are one body in Christ, and individually members one of another" (Rom 12:5). D. A. Carson notes that the unity for which Christ prayed "is not achieved by hunting enthusiastically for the lowest common theological denominator, but by common adherence to the apostolic gospel, by love that is joyfully self-sacrificing, by undaunted commitment to the shared goals of the mission with which Jesus' followers have been charged" (*The Gospel According to John*, The Pillar New Testament Commentary [Grand Rapids: Eerdmans, 1991], 568). By the power of God, believers, united in spiritual life, are also united in purpose, share the same mission, proclaim the same gospel, and manifest the same holiness.

The actual fulfillment of Christ's prayer began with the birth of the church on the day of Pentecost. Suddenly, sovereignly, supernaturally, believers were united by the Spirit into the body of Christ and made one positionally (Acts 2:4). All who have been saved since then have immediately received the baptism of the Holy Spirit, by which they were placed into the body of Christ (1 Cor 12:13). Consequently, there is an extraordinary, supernatural unity in the universal church; it is the "the unity of the Spirit," not created by believers, but preserved by them (Eph 4:3). In Ephesians 4:4–6, Paul lists seven features of that Holy Spirit-created unity.

First, there is "one body," the body of Christ, which is comprised of all believers since the church's inception on the day of Pentecost.

Second, there is "one Spirit," the Holy Spirit, apart from whom no one can believe savingly in

Jesus Christ (1 Cor 12:3). The Spirit is also the agent by which Christ baptizes believers into His body (1 Cor 12:13; cf. Matt 3:11).

Third, there is "one hope," in the promised eternal inheritance guaranteed to every believer by the Holy Spirit (Eph 1:13–14).

Fourth, there is "one Lord," Jesus Christ, who is the sole head of the body (Col 1:18; cf. Acts 4:12; Rom 10:12).

Fifth, there is "one faith," the "faith which was once for all handed down to the saints" (Jude 3); the body of doctrine revealed in the New Testament.

Sixth, there is "one baptism." This probably refers to water baptism, the believer's public confession of faith in Jesus Christ. (Holy Spirit baptism is implied in v. 5.)

Finally, there is "one God and Father of all who is over all and through all and in all." The one true God is the sovereign ruler of everything, including the church.

THE REPRESENTATION OF TRUE UNITY

"even as You, Father, are in Me and I in You, that they also may be in Us.... The glory which You have given Me I have given to them, that they may be one, just as We are one; I in them and You in Me, that they may be perfected in unity ..." (17:21*b*–23*a*)

The unity of nature Christ prayed for reflects that of the Father and the Son, which is expressed in Christ's words **You, Father, are in Me and I in You.** Because of His unity with the Father, Jesus claimed in John 5:16ff. to have the same authority, purpose, power, honor, will, and nature as the Father. That startling claim to full deity and equality with God so outraged His Jewish opponents that they sought to kill Him (5:18; cf. 8:58–59; 10:31–33; 19:7).

The unique intra-Trinitarian relationship of Jesus and the Father forms the pattern for the unity of believers in the church. This prayer reveals five features of that unity the church imitates.

First, the Father and the Son are united in motive; they are equally committed to the glory of God. Jesus began His prayer by saying, "Father, the hour has come; glorify Your Son, that the Son may glorify You" (v. 1), as He had done throughout His ministry (v. 4). In verse 5, He added, "Now, Father, glorify Me together with Yourself, with the glory which I had with You before the world was." Finally, in verse 24 Jesus expressed to the Father His desire that believers would one day "be with Me where I am, so that they may see My glory which You have given Me." In John 7:18 Jesus declared that He was constantly "seeking the glory of the One who sent Him." He did not need to seek His own glory (8:50), because the Father glorified Him (8:54). Both Jesus and the Father were glorified in the raising of Lazarus (11:4). In John 12:28 Jesus prayed, "'Father, glorify Your name.' Then a voice came out of heaven: 'I have both glorified it, and will glorify it again.'" Shortly before His High Priestly Prayer, Jesus had said to the disciples, "Now is the Son of Man glorified, and God is glorified in Him; if God is glorified in Him, God will also glorify Him in Himself, and will glorify Him immediately" (13:31–32). Jesus promised to answer the prayers of His people "so that the Father may be glorified in the Son" (14:13).

The church is also united in a common commitment to the glory of God. "Whether, then, you eat or drink or whatever you do," Paul wrote, "do all to the glory of God" (1 Cor 10:31).

Second, the Father and the Son are united in mission. They share the common goal of redeeming lost sinners and granting them eternal life, as Christ made clear earlier in this prayer:

> Even as You gave Him authority over all flesh, that to all whom You have given Him, He may give eternal life. This is eternal life, that they may know You, the only true God, and Jesus Christ whom You have sent. I glorified You on the earth, having accomplished the work which You have given Me to do.... I have manifested Your name to the men whom You gave Me out of the world; they were Yours and You gave them to Me, and they have kept Your word. (vv. 2–4, 6)

God chose in eternity past to give believers to Christ as a gift of His love, and Christ came to earth to die as a sacrifice for their sins and redeem them. That the church lives to pursue the one goal of evangelizing the lost is clear from Jesus' words in verse 18: "As You sent Me into the world, I also have sent them into the world" (cf. Matt 28:19–20).

Third, the Father and the Son are united in truth. "The words which You gave Me," Jesus said, "I have given to them" (v. 8), while in verse 14 He added, "I have given them Your word." Earlier that evening, Jesus had told the disciples, "The words that I say to you I do not speak on My own initiative, but the Father abiding in Me does His works" (14:10; cf. 3:32–34; 7:16; 8:28, 38, 40; 12:49).

The church is also unified in its commitment to proclaiming the singular truth of God's Word. In Romans 15:5–6, Paul prayed, "Now may the God who gives perseverance and encouragement grant you to be of the same mind with one another according to Christ Jesus, so that with one accord you may with one voice glorify the God and Father of our Lord Jesus Christ" (cf. Acts 2:42, 46; Phil 1:27). Far from dividing the church, a commitment to proclaiming sound doctrine is what defines it.

Fourth, the Father and the Son are united in holiness. In verse 11, Jesus addressed the Father as "Holy Father," and in verse 25 as "righteous Father." The utter holiness of God is expressed throughout the Old and New Testaments. God's holiness is His absolute separation from sin. In Habakkuk 1:13, the prophet declared, "Your eyes are too pure to approve evil, and You can not look on wickedness with favor." In Isaiah's vision of God, the angelic beings cried out, "Holy, Holy, Holy, is the Lord of hosts, the whole earth is full of His glory" (Isa 6:3; cf. Rev 4:8). The writer of Hebrews described Jesus as "holy, innocent, undefiled, separated from sinners" (Heb 7:26). In Revelation 4:8, the heavenly chorus unceasingly cries out, "Holy, holy, holy is the Lord God, the Almighty, who was and who is and who is to come."

When they see believers united in the pursuit of holiness, unbelievers will be drawn to Christ. In Hebrews 12:14, the writer of Hebrews exhorted his readers, "Pursue peace with all men, and the sanctification without which no one will see the Lord." If a church tolerates sin, it not only obscures the glory of Christ it is called to radiate, but also faces the discipline of the Lord of the church (Rev 2:14–16, 20–23).

Finally, the Father and the Son are united in love. In verse 24, Jesus affirmed that the Father had "loved [Him] before the foundation of the world." In John 5:20, Jesus said, "For the Father loves the Son, and shows Him all things that He Himself is doing" (cf. 3:35). Both at His baptism (Matt 3:17) and at the transfiguration (Matt 17:5), the Father declared Jesus to be His beloved Son. Similarly, love is the glue that binds believers together in unity (Col 3:14; cf. 2:2), and it is that love for one another that is the church's ultimate apologetic to the lost world (John 13:34–35).

Though not to the same infinite divine extent, the spiritual life and power that belongs to the Trinity belongs also in some way to believers and is the basis for the church's unity. This is what the Lord meant when He said, **The glory which You have given Me I have given to them, that they may be one, just as we are one; I in them and You in Me, that they may be perfected in unity.** That stunning truth describes believers as those to whom the Son has given glory—that is, aspects of the very divine life that belongs to God. The church's task is to so live as to not obstruct that glory (Matt 5:16).

THE RESULT OF TRUE UNITY

"so that the world may believe that You sent Me.... so that the world may know that You sent Me, and loved them, even as You have loved Me." (17:21*c*–23*b*)

The observable unity of the church authenticates two important realities. First, it gives evidence to **the world** so that it **may believe that** the Father **sent** the Son. That familiar phrase summarizes the plan of redemption, in which God sent Jesus on a mission of salvation "to seek and to save that which was lost" (Luke 19:10). It is so used throughout John's Gospel (e.g., 3:34; 4:34; 5:23, 24, 30, 36, 37, 38; 6:29, 38, 39, 44, 57; 7:16, 18, 28, 29, 33; 8:16, 18, 26, 29, 42; 9:4; 10:36; 11:42; 12:44, 45, 49; 13:20; 14:24; 15:21; 16:5; 17:3, 8, 18, 25; 20:21). Jesus prayed that the visible unity of His church would convince many in the world concerning His divine mission of redemption. The church's unity is the foundation of its evangelism; it demonstrates that Christ is the Savior who transforms lives (cf. John 13:35).

The church's unity also authenticates the Father's love for believers. When unbelievers see believers' love for each other, it offers proof to them that the Father has **loved** those who have believed in His Son. The loving unity of the church made visible is used by God to produce a desire on the part of unbelievers to experience that same love. On the other hand, where there are carnal divisions, strife, backbiting, and quarreling in the church, it drives unbelievers away. Why would they want to be part of such a hypocritical group that is at cross-purposes with itself? The effectiveness of the church's evangelism is devastated by dissension and disputes among its members.

It must be the goal of everyone who is part of the body of Christ through faith in Him to do their part in maintaining the full visibility of the unity that believers possses, as Paul wrote:

> Therefore I, the prisoner of the Lord, implore you to walk in a manner worthy of the calling with which you have been called, with all humility and gentleness, with patience, showing tolerance for one another in love, being diligent to preserve the unity of the Spirit in the bond of peace. (Eph 4:1–3)

06

JESUS PRAYS FOR ALL BELIEVERS—PART 2: THAT THEY WOULD ONE DAY BE REUNITED IN GLORY

JOHN 17:24–26

"Father, I desire that they also, whom You have given Me, be with Me where I am, so that they may see My glory which You have given Me, for You loved Me before the foundation of the world. O righteous Father, although the world has not known You, yet I have known You; and these have known that You sent Me; and I have made Your name known to them, and will make it known, so that the love with which You loved Me may be in them, and I in them." (17:24–26)

I once visited an isolated eastern city in the former Soviet Union, where I met with fifteen hundred impoverished Christians. They were the descendants of exiles, and they and their ancestors had suffered terribly under Soviet oppression for three quarters of a century. Their poverty was so severe that they had to work hard every day just to put food on the table. The subject that was most on their heart was their future in the glory of heaven. I had the privilege of teaching them about that from Scripture for several hours, and many were so overcome that they wept with joy.

Their response was strikingly different from that of many Christians in the West, who have things so good that they do not know what it is to long for heaven. As a result, they live as if going to heaven would be an unwelcome intrusion into their busy schedules—an interruption of their career goals or vacation plans.

They do not want to see heaven until they have enjoyed all the pleasures the world has to offer. When they have seen it all and done it all, or when age or sickness hinder their ability to enjoy those pleasures, then they will be ready for heaven. While it is true that, as the old spiritual put it, "Everybody talkin' 'bout heaven ain't goin' there," it is also true that everybody going to heaven is not talking about it.

When the church loses its focus on heaven, it becomes self-indulgent and self-centered, materialistic and worldly, spiritually weak and lethargic. The pleasures and comforts of this present world consume too much of its time and energy. Believers forget that this world is not their true home, that they are "aliens and strangers" (1 Pet 2:11; cf. Heb 11:13) here, that their "citizenship is in heaven" (Phil 3:20), and that "here we do not have a lasting city, but we are seeking the city which is to come" (Heb 13:14). The church is increasingly in danger not of being so heavenly minded that it is no earthly good, but rather of being so earthly minded that it is no heavenly good.

A worldly minded church is the result of a disobedient church. The Lord Jesus Christ commanded His followers, "Store up for yourselves treasures in heaven, where neither moth nor rust destroys, and where thieves do not break in or steal; for where your treasure is, there your heart will be also" (Matt 6:20–21). "Therefore if you have been raised up with

Christ," Paul wrote, "keep seeking the things above, where Christ is, seated at the right hand of God" (Col 3:1). The apostle John warned believers,

> Do not love the world nor the things in the world. If anyone loves the world, the love of the Father is not in him. For all that is in the world, the lust of the flesh and the lust of the eyes and the boastful pride of life, is not from the Father, but is from the world. The world is passing away, and also its lusts; but the one who does the will of God lives forever. (1 John 2:15–17)

Godly men have always longed for heaven. In the Old Testament David expressed his heart's yearning for heaven when he wrote, "In Your presence is fullness of joy; in Your right hand there are pleasures forever" (Ps 16:11). In the New Testament Paul wrote to the Philippians of his "desire to depart and be with Christ, for that is very much better" (Phil 1:23), while in 2 Corinthians 5:8 he declared his preference "to be absent from the body and to be at home with the Lord." In his triumphant epitaph, Paul wrote to Timothy,

> For I am already being poured out as a drink offering, and the time of my departure has come. I have fought the good fight, I have finished the course, I have kept the faith; in the future there is laid up for me the crown of righteousness, which the Lord, the righteous Judge, will award to me on that day; and not only to me, but also to all who have loved His appearing. (2 Tim 4:6–8)

Like David and Paul, all Christians should long for heaven, since everything precious to them is there. Their Father is there. Jesus taught believers to pray, "Our Father who is in heaven, hallowed be Your name" (Matt 6:9; cf. vv. 1, 14, 32; 5:48; 18:14; 23:9; Luke 11:13). Their fellow believers who have died are there. The writer of Hebrews described the "general assembly and church of the firstborn who are enrolled in heaven, and ... the spirits of the righteous made perfect" (Heb 12:23). Their names are recorded there. In Luke 10:20, Jesus told the disciples, "Do not rejoice in this, that the spirits are subject to you, but rejoice that your names are recorded in heaven" (cf. Phil 4:3; Rev 3:5; 13:8; 17:8; 20:12, 15; 21:27). As noted earlier, their citizenship is there (Phil 3:20). Their inheritance is there. Peter described it as "an inheritance which is imperishable and undefiled and will not fade away, reserved in heaven for you" (1 Pet 1:4). Their holiness is there (Rev 21:27; 22:3, 14–15). Their eternal reward is there. In Matthew 5:12, Jesus exhorted believers, "Rejoice and be glad, for your reward in heaven is great," while in 6:19–21 He spoke of believers' treasure being in heaven.

Most important of all, their Savior is there, "standing at the right hand of God" (Acts 7:55, 56; cf. Rom 8:34; Col 3:1; Heb 1:3; 8:1; 10:12; 12:2; 1 Pet 3:22). He has gone there to prepare a place for them (John 14:1–3), so they can be with Him forever, sharing rich fellowship with Him and worshiping Him. Jesus Himself is the glory of heaven.

The reality that believers will be reunited in heaven with Christ and each other is the subject of the last part of the Lord's High Priestly Prayer. Verses 24–26 describe the fellowship of future glory, the focus of future glory, and the foretaste of future glory.

THE FELLOWSHIP OF FUTURE GLORY

"Father, I desire that they also, whom You have given Me, be with Me where I am ..." (17:24*a*)

This passionate plea that those **whom** the Father has **given** to Him might **be with** Him in His eternal glory in heaven is the final petition of Christ's prayer.

Humanly speaking, there is nothing to warrant such a staggering, overwhelming privilege. Christians, as Paul reminded the Corinthians, are "not many wise according to the flesh, not many mighty, not many noble" (1 Cor 1:26). Even worse, they were God's enemies (Rom 5:10),

> dead in [their] trespasses and sins, in which [they] formerly walked according to the course of this world, according to the prince of the power of the air, of the spirit that is now working in the sons of disobedience. Among them [they] too all formerly lived in the lusts of [their] flesh, indulging

> the desires of the flesh and of the mind, and were by nature children of wrath, even as the rest. (Eph 2:1–3)

They were "separate from Christ, excluded from the commonwealth of Israel, and strangers to the covenants of promise, having no hope and without God in the world" (Eph 2:12), having "sinned and fall[en] short of the glory of God" (Rom 3:23).

But the marvelous truth of redemption is that

> God, being rich in mercy, because of His great love with which He loved us, even when we were dead in our transgressions, made us alive together with Christ (by grace you have been saved), and raised us up with Him, and seated us with Him in the heavenly places in Christ Jesus, so that in the ages to come He might show the surpassing riches of His grace in kindness toward us in Christ Jesus. (Eph 2:4–7)

God, Paul wrote to the Christians at Rome,

> demonstrates His own love toward us, in that while we were yet sinners, Christ died for us. Much more then, having now been justified by His blood, we shall be saved from the wrath of God through Him. For if while we were enemies we were reconciled to God through the death of His Son, much more, having been reconciled, we shall be saved by His life. (Rom 5:8–10)

Not only does God forgive repentant sinners, but He also adopts them as His children (Rom 8:15; Gal 4:5; Eph 1:5). That truth prompted the apostle John to exclaim in wonder, "See how great a love the Father has bestowed on us, that we would be called children of God; and such we are" (1 John 3:1). The glorification of believers in heaven is the ultimate goal of the plan of salvation: "For those whom He foreknew, He also predestined to become conformed to the image of His Son, so that He would be the firstborn among many brethren; and these whom He predestined, He also called; and these whom He called, He also justified; and these whom He justified, He also glorified" (Rom 8:29–30).

Jesus' request was in perfect harmony with God's purpose in choosing believers before the foundation of the world (Eph 1:4), inscribing their names in the Book of Life, and giving them to the Son as gifts of His love (John 6:37, 39). True prayer is always consistent with God's will. Jesus taught His followers to pray to God, "Your kingdom come. Your will be done, on earth as it is in heaven" (Matt 6:10).

But the Lord's request was more than merely a plea that the Father's will be done; it also expressed His **desire** (*thelō*; "to wish," "to desire," "to want"). It is not difficult to understand believers wanting to be with Him; but it staggers the imagination to realize that He wants them to be with Him.

The phrase **they ... whom You have given Me** expresses again the reason that believers are special to Christ: they are a love gift to Him from the Father. It is the Lord's most affectionate way of referring to believers when addressing the Father (vv. 2, 6, 9; cf. 6:37, 39, 10:29; 18:9). The church is His bride (Rev 19:7; cf. 2 Cor 11:2; Eph 5:22–24), betrothed to Him by His Father.

Christ's specific request for those given Him by the Father, that they might **be with Me where I am,** further expressed His desire for eternal fellowship with them. He wants all of those chosen for Him in eternity past to be with Him where He now is—heaven. In John 14:3, Jesus revealed His purpose in bringing believers to heaven: "If I go and prepare a place for you, I will come again and receive you to Myself, that where I am, there you may be also." In John 12:26, He promised, "If anyone serves Me, he must follow Me; and where I am, there My servant will be also."

The Lord's use of the present tense, **where I am,** obviously does not refer to His location in Jerusalem on the way to Gethsemane. Such a request would have been pointless, since the disciples were already with Him. Further, in this section of His prayer, Christ looked beyond the eleven disciples to all who would believe in Him in the future through their ministry. Jesus was not speaking of where He was at that moment, but where He would soon be. He was so certain that He would be returning to heaven that He spoke of that future event in the present tense, as if it had already happened (cf. v. 11).

What will make heaven so glorious for believers is not its gates of pearl, or streets of gold, but the presence of the Lamb. Their supreme joy will be to "dwell in the house of the Lord forever" (Ps 23:6), experiencing perfect, intimate, holy fellowship with Him and all the saints forever.

THE FOCUS OF FUTURE GLORY

"so that they may see My glory which You have given Me ..." (17:24*b*)

Jesus also asked the Father that His followers might **see** His **glory which** the Father had **given** Him. It is true that in Christ's incarnation "we saw His glory, glory as of the only begotten from the Father" (John 1:14). But that glory was veiled in His flesh (Phil 2:5–8). Only in heaven will it be fully manifested to His people when they "see Him just as He is" (1 John 3:2; cf. 1 Cor 13:12; Phil 2:9–11).

In God's gracious plan, believers will not only see Christ's glory, but also share it: "For our citizenship is in heaven," Paul wrote to the Philippians, "from which also we eagerly wait for a Savior, the Lord Jesus Christ; who will transform the body of our humble state into conformity with the body of His glory, by the exertion of the power that He has even to subject all things to Himself" (Phil 3:20–21; cf. Rom 8:29; 1 Cor 15:49;

1 John 3:2). Throughout all eternity the song of the redeemed as they behold the glory of the Lord Jesus Christ will be, "Worthy is the Lamb that was slain to receive power and riches and wisdom and might and honor and glory and blessing.... To Him who sits on the throne, and to the Lamb, be blessing and honor and glory and dominion forever and ever" (Rev 5:12–13).

This request complements the statement the Lord made back in verse 22: "The glory which You have given Me I have given to them." In the incarnation, Christ had manifested "His glory, glory as of the only begotten from the Father" (John 1:14; cf. 2:11). Believers also receive Christ's glory through His indwelling of them through the Holy Spirit (vv. 23, 26; 14:20, 23). In that sense, they have His glory—His attributes and essence—within them.

But the glory of which Christ speaks here is the visible manifestation of the fullness of His glory that believers will one day see in heaven. In the incarnation, Christ's glory was partially veiled (cf. Phil 2:7). But when Jesus returned to heaven, the Father restored that fullness of glory to Him, as He had requested in verse 5: "Now, Father, glorify Me together with Yourself, with the glory which I had with You before the world was."

Believers will enter the fullness of Christ's glorious presence when they die (or at the rapture, if they are alive at that time). To see God after death has always been the hope of the saints. In Psalm 11:7, David expressed his confidence that "the upright will behold His face," while in Psalm 17:15 he wrote, "As for me, I shall behold Your face in righteousness; I will be satisfied with Your likeness when I awake." Jesus pronounced the pure in heart "Blessed ... for they shall see God" (Matt 5:8). John wrote that one day believers "will see Him just as He is" (1 John 3:2), while Revelation 22:3–4 reveals that in heaven, "There will no longer be any curse; and the throne of God and of the Lamb will be in it, and His bond-servants will serve Him; they will see His face, and His name will be on their foreheads." So overwhelming will the manifestation of Christ's glory be that the only possible response will be praise:

> Then I looked, and I heard the voice of many angels around the throne and the living creatures and the elders; and the number of them was myriads of myriads, and thousands of thousands, saying with a loud voice, "Worthy is the Lamb that was slain to receive power and riches and wisdom and might and honor and glory and blessing." And every created thing which is in heaven and on the earth and under the earth and on the sea, and all things in them, I heard saying, "To Him who sits on the throne, and to the Lamb, be blessing and honor and glory and dominion forever and ever." And the four living creatures kept saying, "Amen." And the elders fell down and worshiped. (Rev 5:11–14)

All of the blessings believers will one day experience in heaven flow from the reality that the Father **loved** the Son **before the foundation of the world.** From all eternity, the Father and Son enjoyed perfect fellowship (John 1:1), love, and shared glory (17:5). As indicated throughout this prayer, based on that mutual love, the Father chose a people (Eph 1:4), gave them to the Son, and prepared an eternal kingdom for them (Matt 25:34) where they will behold His glory forever.

THE FORETASTE OF FUTURE GLORY

"O righteous Father, although the world has not known You, yet I have known You; and these have known that You sent Me; and I have made Your name known to them, and will make it known, so that the love with which You loved Me may be in them, and I in them." (17:25–26)

The closing verses of this magnificent prayer exude Christ's confidence that the **righteous Father** (cf. v. 11; Deut 32:4; Pss 7:9; 11:7; 50:6; 71:19; 116:5; Isa 5:16; 45:21; Rom 3:22, 25; Rev 15:3) would grant His requests (cf. John 11:42). God is **righteous** in everything He does (Ps 145:17); His judgments (Pss 19:9; 119:7; Rom 2:5), deeds (Ps 103:6), ordinances (Ps 119:62), and Word (Ps 119:123) are righteous.

Jesus reiterated the point He had made earlier in verse 9. His requests were not for **the world,** which **has not known** the Father and hence has no right to receive His special care or the Son's intercession. Apart from faith in Jesus Christ, sinners face only eternal judgment. In John 3:18, Jesus warned, "He who does not believe has been judged already, because he has not believed in the name of the only begotten Son of God," while in 3:36 John the Baptist added, "He who believes in the Son has eternal life; but he who does not obey the Son will not see life, but the wrath of God abides on him."

Not only had Jesus perfectly **known** the Father from all eternity (Matt 11:27; John 1:1, 18; 7:29; 8:55; 10:15), but He had also **made** His **name known to** His followers, who had **known that** the Father had **sent** Him (v. 6; Matt 11:27; John 1:18; 15:15; 1 Tim 2:5). The Lord's mission was to lead lost sinners into a personal relationship with God (Luke 19:10), which comes only through the knowledge of Him (John 17:3, cf. 14:6). Jesus initially makes the Father known at the moment of salvation, continues to **make** Him **known** to believers through the process of sanctification, and finally ushers them into the Father's heavenly presence at their glorification. His goal is **that** even now they might experience **the love with which** the Father **loved** Christ, and by knowing "the love of Christ which surpasses knowledge, that [they might] be filled up to all the fullness of God" (Eph 3:19). God's love is poured out on believers at salvation (Rom 5:5), continues in them as Christ indwells them (cf. John 14:23), and is fulfilled perfectly in them in heaven.

Christ's requests in this, the greatest prayer ever prayed, may be summed up in seven words. The Lord prayed for believers' preservation ("Holy Father, keep them in Your name," v. 11); jubilation ("that they may have My joy made full in themselves," v. 13); liberation ("keep them from the evil one," v. 15); sanctification ("sanctify them in the truth; Your word is truth," v. 17); unification ("that they may all be one," v. 21); association ("Father, I desire that they also, whom You have given Me, be with Me where I am," v. 24); and glorification ("that they may see My glory," v. 24).

BIBLIOGRAPHY

Baxter, Richard. *The Saints' Everlasting Rest.* In *The Practical Works of Richard Baxter.* Grand Rapids: Baker, 1981.

Boice, James Montgomery. *The Gospel of John.* Grand Rapids: Zondervan, 1985.

Borchert, Gerald L. *John 12–21.* The New American Commentary. Nashville: Broadman & Holman, 2002.

Carson, D. A. *The Gospel According to John.* The Pillar New Testament Commentary. Grand Rapids: Eerdmans, 1991.

Gaebelein, A. C. *The Gospel of John.* Wheaton, IL: Van Kampen Press, 1936.

Godet, Frederic. *Commentary on John's Gospel.* Grand Rapids: Kregel, 1978.

Greene, Oliver. *The Gospel According to John.* Vol. 3. Greenville, SC: The Gospel Hour, 1966.

Köstenberger, Andreas. *John.* Baker Exegetical Commentary on the New Testament. Grand Rapids: Baker, 2004.

Lenski, R. C. H. *The Interpretation of St. John's Gospel.* Minneapolis: Augsburg, 1943.

MacArthur, John. "Divine Immutability and the Doctrines of Grace." In Steven J. Lawson. *Foundations of Grace.* Orlando, FL: Reformation Trust, 2006.

MacArthur, John. *John 1–11.* The MacArthur New Testament Commentary. Chicago: Moody Publishers, 2006.

Meyer, F. B. *Gospel of John.* Grand Rapids: Zondervan, 1952.

Mitchell, Curtis C. *Praying Jesus' Way.* Old Tappan, NJ: Revell, 1977.

Morris, Leon. *The Gospel According to John.* The New International Commentary on the New Testament. Grand Rapids: Eerdmans, 1995.

Phillips, John. *Exploring the Gospel of John.* Grand Rapids: Kregel, 1989.

Reynolds, H. R. *St. John.* The Pulpit Commentary. Edited by H. D. M. Spence and Joseph S. Exell. Grand Rapids: Eerdmans, 1981.

Schreiner, Thomas. "Penal Substitution View." In *The Nature of the Atonement: Four Views.* Edited by James Beilby and Paul R. Eddy. Downers Grove, IL: InterVarsity, 2006.

Spurgeon, Charles. "Prayer—the Forerunner of Mercy." In *The New Park Street Pulpit.* Pasadena, TX: Pilgrim, 1981.

Tenney, Merrill C. "The Gospel of John." In *The Expositor's Bible Commentary.* Edited by Frank E. Gaebelein. Grand Rapids: Zondervan, 1981.

Watson, Thomas. *The Godly Man's Picture.* Edinburgh: Banner of Truth, 1992.

Witherington, Ben III. *John's Wisdom.* Louisville: Westminster John Knox Press, 1995.

INDEXES

INDEX OF SCRIPTURE

INDEX OF SUBJECTS

JOHN MACARTHUR PUBLISHING GROUP
LOS ANGELES, CALIFORNIA